SCAMS, SHAMS, AND FLIMFLAMS

From King Tut to Elvis Lives

SCAMS, SHAMS, AND FLIMFLAMS

From King Tut to Elvis Lives

VOLUME 2

Gordon Stein and Marie J. MacNee

AN IMPRINT OF GALE RESEARCH INC.

Scams, Shams, and Flimflams:
From King Tut to Elvis Lives

Gordon Stein and Marie J. MacNee

STAFF

Kathleen L. Witman, *Assistant Developmental Editor*

Carol DeKane Nagel, *Developmental Editor*

Thomas L. Romig, *U•X•L Publisher*

Barbara A. Wallace, *Permissions Associate*
(Pictures)

Margaret A. Chamberlain , *Permissions Supervisor*
(Pictures)

Mary Kelley, *Production Associate*

Evi Seoud, *Assistant Production Manager*

Mary Beth Trimper, *Production Director*

Mary Krzewinski, *Page and Cover Designer*

Cynthia Baldwin, *Art Director*

Terry Colon, *Illustrator*

Linda Mahoney, *Typesetter*

Library of Congress Cataloging-in-Publication Data
Scams, shams, and flimflams : from King Tut to Elvis lives / Gordon Stein and Marie J. MacNee.
     p.   cm.
  "Volume I"--CIP t.p.
  Includes index.
  ISBN 0-8103-9784-6 (set) : $38.00. -- ISBN 0-8103-9785-4 (v. 1). -- ISBN 0-8103-9786-2 (v. 2)
     1. Impostors and imposture--Juvenile literature. 2. Fraud--Juvenile literature. 3. Swindlers and swindling--Juvenile literature. 4. Deception--Juvenile literature. [1. Impostors and imposture. 2. Swindlers and swindling.] I. MacNee, Marie J. II. Title.
HV6751.S7 1994
363.1'63--dc20
                                                                                              94-15067
                                                                                                    CIP
                                                                                                    AC

This book is printed on acid-free paper that meets the minimum requirements of American National Standard for Information Sciences—Permanence Paper for Printed Library Materials, ANSI Z39.48-1984.

Printed in the United States of America

Published simultaneously in the United Kingdom
by Gale Research International Limited
(An affiliated company of Gale Research Inc.)

CONTENTS

II
SAINTS, SPIRITS, AND
SUPERNATURAL SCAMS   29

III
HAUNTED HOUSES, CRYPTIC CURSES, AND FORECASTS OF THE FARAWAY FUTURE 61

TALL TALES OF DOOM AND GLOOM 62

IV
GLOBE-TROTTING AND GALLIVANTING 77

CRAFTY SAILORS AND SLY EXPLORERS 78

V
MILITARY MANEUVERS 89

SLICK SOLDIERS AND SLIPPERY SPYMASTERS 90

VOLUME 2

VIII
HEROES, BAD GUYS, AND IMPOSTORS   135

IX
YOU CAN'T BELIEVE EVERYTHING YOU READ 171

X
SEEING ISN'T ALWAYS BELIEVING 183

INTRODUCTION

Haunted houses, lake monsters, flying saucers, and deadly death rays. Who hasn't heard of the Bermuda Triangle, the Loch Ness Monster, or the Amityville horror? Yet how many people know the *real* story? Was Silence Dogood Ben Franklin's feminine pen name? Has Elvis Presley booked a return engagement to the world of the living? Is the Loch Ness Monster really an otter? Enquiring minds want to know.

SCAMS, SHAMS, AND FLIMFLAMS BLOWS THE WHISTLE ON 100 HOAXES!

There's no denying it: Weird stuff happens, and sometimes it's *made* to happen. Wouldn't it be great if there were somewhere to find out how The Man Who Never Was managed to fool the Nazis during World War II? How a guy with humongous wooden feet made it look like Bigfoot had been waltzing through the woods? How a psychic "predicted" the president would be shot? If you've got to know how they did it—and maybe even *why* they did it—then look no further: *Scams, Shams, and Flimflams* will tell you everything you always wanted to know about bogus Blue Laws, big-footed beasts, biorhythms, and more.

What exactly is a hoax?

Cons, humbugs, ripoffs, scams, shams, and flimflams—hoaxes by any other name—involve fooling at least *some* people *some* of the time. *Webster's Unabridged Dictionary* (10th ed.) defines a hoax as "an act intended to trick or dupe; something accepted or established by fraud or fabrication." Well, that's a start. Guido Franch was definitely up to mischief when he asked automobile companies to pay him $10 million for a secret fuel formula they could neither see nor test before they paid him. Ben Franklin had a practical joke in mind when he announced— six years prematurely—that a rival almanac writer had died. And Daniel Dunglas Home used more than a little deception to fool people into believing he was floating in thin air.

A successful hoax must be at least a *little* bit believable. Hitler *could* have escaped from his bunker on April 30, 1945. Jack the Ripper *might* have been a doctor who routinely executed the witnesses to a royal scandal. The boy King Tut *might* have cursed all who crashed his kingly catacomb. Then again, maybe not. Often, a good hoax relies on the listener's preconceived notions. Think about it: How many people would have spotted a single sea serpent in Scotland if no one had ever heard of the Loch Ness Monster? Most hoaxes work because *somebody somewhere* is ready, willing, and eager to believe the less than believable.

Does a hoaxer want the hoax to be discovered?

Never; always; sometimes. It depends. Some hoaxes bloom *after* they've been discovered. Take, for instance, George Plimpton's piece about pitching prodigy Sidd Finch that appeared in an April 1 issue of *Sports Illustrated*. The fact is, there *was* no Sidd Finch; that was the point. If no one had discovered that Finch was a phantom, then the article—filled with phoney photographs and bogus biography—would have no point.

At other times, publicity destroys the hoax. Ferdinand Demara, known as "The Great Impostor," had quite a career as a surgeon, a priest, a naval officer, and a number of other occupations that struck his fancy. When *Life* magazine published a portrait of the impostor, however, Demara's career options were soon severely limited.

What isn't a hoax?

Are hoaxes sometimes motivated by financial gain? You betcha. But a hoax—unlike a swindle—is not *based* on the financial return. The master forger Hans van Meegeren, for example, managed to earn a tidy sum by forging the works of famous artists. The money, however, was simply a perk. The second-hand artist had quite another motive in mind: He wanted to force a group of art critics to dine on humble pie—and he succeeded, in spades.

A hoaxer, without exception, *purposely intends* to deceive people. Carlos Allende, who called his UFO stories "the craziest [sic] pack of lies" he ever told, was a card-carrying hoaxer. But not everyone with a wacky take on reality is. Not every tale of Venusian visitors and Elvis encounters is perpetrated by a hoaxer. Some are created by certified cranks—eccentrics who *believe* that what they're saying is *true*.

Not every hoax started out as a hoax. Christopher Columbus had no idea when he died that his grave would inspire centuries of squabbling. Nor did Nostradamus know that his predictions—intended to cover local events in the immediate future—would be used by a Nazi astronomer to predict Germany's victory in World War II. Hoaxes sometimes gather momentum as time goes by.

What you'll find in the books

In two volumes, *Scams, Shams, and Flimflams* offers more than 100 descriptions of well-known hoaxes. The first volume, divided into six sections, includes hoaxes having to do with weird creatures and visitors from beyond; saints, spirits, and the supernatural; curses and predictions; exploration; military maneuvers; and outrageous rules. The second volume, also divided into six sections, includes scores of other hoaxes involving science and medicine; impostors; literature and the arts; entertainment; and sports. Each entry includes interesting background information, an account of how the hoax was played out, how it was discovered, and finally, how it impacted the world. You'll also find 65 photographs that bring the hoaxes to life, and 16 line drawings, too. An index—closing both volumes—provides quick access to names, subjects, and individual hoaxes.

So if you always wanted to be an expert on laws against kissing, if you have a burning need to know about the Hope Diamond curse, or if you just want to read about weird stuff ... inquire within.

Comments and Suggestions

We welcome your comments on this work as well as your suggestions for hoaxes to be featured in future editions of *Scams, Shams, and Flimflams*. Please write: Editors, *Scams, Shams, and Flimflams*, U•X•L, 835 Penobscot Bldg., Detroit, Michigan 48226-4094; or call toll-free: 1-800-877-4253; or fax 313-961-6348.

PICTURE CREDITS

Photographs and illustrations appearing in *Scams, Shams, and Flim-flams* were received from the following sources:

Brown Brothers: pp. 4, 13, 68, 131, 137, 173; AP/Wide World Photos: pp. 7, 11, 17, 37, 39, 43, 63, 66, 75, 82, 121, 125, 144, 149, 151, 169, 202, 203, 211; courtesy of Gordon Stein: pp. 14, 66, 91, 95, 127, 192, 209; Mary Evans Picture Library: pp. 15, 24, 54, 72, 93; Archive Photos: pp. 21, 200; The Bettmann Archive: pp. 34, 83, 143, 146, 157, 161, 163, 177, 205; UPI/Bettmann: pp. 45, 48, 51, 79, 101, 141, 158, 167, 168, 191; Courtesy of John Beloff: p 55; Courtesy of *Louisville Courier Journal*: p. 70; Minnesota Historical Society: p. 87; Culver Pictures, Inc.: p. 138; *Lane H. Stewart/Sports Illustrated:* p. 214.

Weird Science,
Bad Medicine,
and Illegitimate
Inventions

Fraud in the Halls of Science

HOAX CHAIN REACTIONS

Because the work of scientists builds on previous work, any fraud that goes undetected may have disastrous results when it is finally revealed. If a published paper is found to have been fraudulent, it has to be publicly retracted; more importantly, any research inspired by the fraudulent paper has to be redone.

DARSEE, SUMMERLIN, AND RESEARCH FRAUD

John Roland Darsee was a brilliant young physician who was working at one of the hospitals affiliated with Harvard Medical School in Boston in 1981. Known for the tremendous number of research papers he produced, Darsee studied the heart muscle of heart-attack patients. His research indicated that much of the injured heart muscle could be restored to function after a heart attack.

William T. Summerlin worked at the Sloan-Kettering Institute for Cancer Research in New York City in 1974. At a meeting of science writers, Summerlin told journalists that "after human skin is maintained in organ culture for four to six weeks, it becomes universally transplantable without rejection." It looked like the major obstacle to transplantation had been overcome. As it turns out, Summerlin and Darsee each did considerable damage to biomedical research by submitting fraudulent accounts of their research experiments.

Scientists Fake Results of Ground-Breaking Research!

Although John Darsee obviously worked quite hard, many people, especially his coworkers, wondered how he could produce such a large volume of research—research that would normally be very complicated and time-consuming. One evening in May 1981, they secretly watched as Darsee forged raw data for an experiment that he was about to submit for publication. It seems that when his supervisor asked for the raw

data, Darsee went into a laboratory and proceeded to make up the data. Although he confessed when he was confronted about the phoney results, Darsee claimed that this was the only experiment he had ever faked.

Stripped of his Harvard appointment, Darsee was still allowed to continue working in the laboratory; his coworkers, however, were still suspicious. Darsee also continued to contribute abstracts and papers. Part of his funding had come from the National Institutes of Health (NIH), and NIH investigators began to suspect that the fraud might have been more widespread.

A blue ribbon panel was formed at Harvard in early December 1981, in order to look into the matter. What they found did not look good: Darsee could not produce any raw data for studies he had conducted after his first year at the laboratory—that is to say, after his work was less carefully supervised.

THE "GOLDEN HANDS" HOAXER

Mark Spector made up college degrees that he didn't have, and he almost earned a doctorate from Cornell University in 1981. Because only he could get some experiments to work, he was known for his "golden hands" in the laboratory. This should have aroused suspicion, but it didn't—at first.

Spector researched the purification of a type of ATPase, the enzyme that pumps ions out of cells, converting ATP to ADP in the process. This is an important reaction in cellular metabolism, and Spector apparently showed that cancer cells were not able to perform the process well.

Spector's later work provided a basis for a unified theory about the cause of cancer. Then something odd was discovered: Radioactive iodine was found in the mixture, although no iodine whatsoever should have been present. As it turned out, some of the radioactive bands that identified the separated-out enzymes were due to the radioactive iodine that had been added.

When Spector's notebooks were inspected for raw data, they were full of data that had been written in, without printouts from the electronic equipment that was analyzing the samples. His fraud discovered, Spector was dismissed from Cornell. He didn't receive his Ph.D., and it came to light that his B.A. and his M.S. degrees were fakes.

The blue ribbon panel's report. The panel's report cleared Harvard of any blame for having allowed Darsee to continue his research in the lab for six months after his initial fraud was discovered. As it turned out, two studies conducted during that six-month period contained data that were "highly suspect," and Darsee was forced to resign from the Sloan-Kettering laboratory.

Still more fraud lurked in the halls of science. After he received his M.D. from Indiana University, and before he arrived at Harvard, Darsee spent a number of years at Emory University in Atlanta, Georgia. After Darsee's forced resignation, Emory opened an investigation of his work. This was no small task: During his five years at Emory, Darsee had written ten papers and forty-five abstracts.

Most of Darsee's publications were suspect and had to be retracted; only two papers and two abstracts were allowed to stand. What's more, Darsee had apparently put the names of Emory scientists on his abstracts as coauthors, without their knowledge. It seems none of the "coauthors" had objected—that is, if they ever found out.

Suspicious breakthroughs in transplantation. Much of William Summerlin's work involved the transplantation of rabbit corneas. But his colleagues were suspicious: The eyes of the rabbits who were supposed to have received transplants were a bit too perfect.

Summerlin also produced two white mice with black patches on their skin. He told his supervisor, Dr. Robert Good, that the dark patches were areas of skin that had been transplanted from black-skinned mice. It seems that isn't exactly how Summerlin had created the black patches: He had, in fact, inked the black patches on the mice with a felt-tip pen. When a lab assistant noticed the fakery and reported it to his superiors, Summerlin was immediately suspended from the laboratory.

Medical leave for exhaustion. Dr. Lewis Thomas, the president of Sloan-Kettering, set up a formal investigation. Having reviewed Summerlin's work, the investigating committee decided to terminate Summerlin's relationship with Sloan-Kettering. Good, on the other hand, was cleared of any role in the fraud.

In the end, Summerlin, who claimed that he had been forced into fraud because of the intense pressure on him to produce, was given a period of medical leave, with pay, so that he could recover from what was called "exhaustion."

RORVIK AND THE CLONING OF A MAN

David Rorvik was a science journalist who had a respectable reputation. When he published *In His Image: The Cloning of a Man* in 1978, the public was fascinated. Many people accepted Rorvik's claim that a human being had been cloned, but the scientific community was not convinced.

Journalist Discovers Boy Cloned in Tropical Laboratory!

Scientists were reluctant to believe Rorvik. They knew that technology was not sufficiently advanced to produce a human clone—an individual who is grown from a single cell from the parent and is genetically identical to the parent. To make matters worse, Rorvik did not supply adequate documentation to convince the scientists that human cloning had occurred.

In his book, Rorvik claimed to have received a phone call from an elderly millionaire called "Max." Rorvik had previously been the science editor for *Time* magazine, and Max was familiar with Rorvik's writings about human reproduction and cloning.

The millionaire, it seems, was interested in cloning himself, and was willing to shell out a tidy sum to do it. With millions of dollars as his incentive, Rorvik found a willing scientist, "Darwin," who was a gynecologist (someone who deals with the diseases and health of women).

Darwin and Rorvik set up a lab in a tropical country where native women were to supply eggs and would attempt to carry the embryo clone to term (until it was ready to be born). The nucleus of a cell from Max's body was transferred to a cell without a nucleus from

BIOCHEMICAL BREAKTHROUGH OR BUST?

Rorvik claimed that, to speed up the success rate of cloning a human, the experiment included a number of "serial transfers" of one nucleus to another. Scientists know that this can't be done because only a colony of cells would exist. Yet Rorvik claimed that "biochemical breakthroughs" allowed the serial transfers to succeed.

If these breakthroughs had really taken place, modern medicine would be able to tackle a number of thorny problems, such as cancer, tissue regeneration, and transplantation. Could a scientist and a science journalist working in isolation in a small tropical lab have the equipment, technique, and knowledge to accomplish in one short period what thousands of scientists over the decades have tried unsuccessfully to do? The Nobel Prize committee doesn't seem to think so.

TEST TUBE COLONIES AND THE ZONA PELLUCIDA

In order to introduce the new nucleus from the donor's cell into the egg cell, the outer layer of the egg cell, called the "zona pellucida," would have to be stripped off. An egg stripped of its zona pellucida cannot survive implantation in a uterus. Although it will grow in a test tube, it will only produce colonies of similar cells; it will **not** produce an embryo.

"Sparrow," the selected "mother." When Sparrow carried the embryo to term and delivered a boy in the United States, millionaire Max had a perfect clone of himself.

A lawsuit against Rorvik's publisher. In his book, Rorvik mentioned Derek Bromhall, a British scientist, as the man who had developed the scientific basis for cloning; the public took this as proof for the claim that a human cloning had occurred. In 1978, however, Bromhall sued J. B. Lippincott, the publisher of Rorvik's cloning book, claiming—in federal court—that his reputation had been harmed by the book. Bromhall accused Rorvik of quoting from his doctoral dissertation, which explored the possibility of human cloning. What's more, Rorvik was not authorized to quote the scientist's research.

Weird Science, Bad Medicine, and Illegitimate Inventions

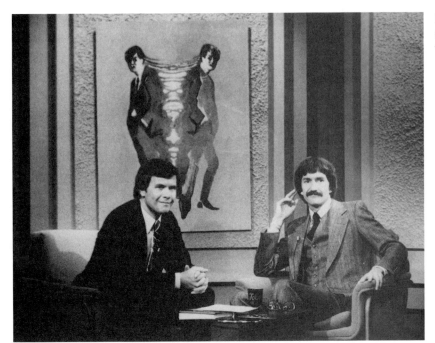

David Rorvik appearing on the *Today* show with host Tom Brokaw in 1978.

Bromhall pointed out a number of problems with Rorvik's book. For instance, the cloning process that Rorvik described (very vaguely) was theoretically impossible as it was outlined in the book. It seems that Rorvik did not understand cloning research, and many of the errors in his book stemmed from this lack of understanding.

Of frogs and men. In the mid-1960s, scientists had been successful in cloning a frog. Cloning a human being, however—as Bromhall noted—posed a different set of problems. A frog's egg is much larger than a human egg and is therefore easier to work with.

Rorvik claimed that the nucleus of the donor egg was removed by treating it with the chemical Cytochalasin B. The trouble is, although this chemical will remove the nucleus (or "enucleate") some cells, it will not enucleate an egg cell.

More reason to question Rorvik's book. Rorvik's book was printed by the publishing company's trade division, not by the medical division. While the trade division simply accepted Rorvik's reputation, the medical division could have had outside experts review the manuscript. What's more, Rorvik's timing was off. Several months after the cloning was supposed to have been done, the journalist was still trying to get information from Bromhall about his cloning methods.

NO EVIDENCE OF
A MIRACLE

Rorvik eventually claimed that the cloned boy developed a "defect"—a convenient way to avoid having to produce the medical miracle in public. Although the millionaire donor had agreed to blood tests, they were conducted under secret conditions, and the results could not be tied to any particular individual.

Only a blood test of father and son—at the same time and in the same room—could definitively prove that their blood was identical. No such test was ever conducted.

A fraud and a hoax. Based on this evidence and on the testimony of court experts, Judge John Fullam ruled that the book was "a fraud and a hoax." He said that the plaintiff had finally and conclusively established that "the cloning described in the book never took place" and that "all of the characters mentioned in the book, other than the defendant Rorvik, have and had no real existence." In 1982, Bromhall settled his case against Rorvik out of court, for an undisclosed sum. Part of the settlement agreement required Rorvik (who continued to deny that the book was a hoax) to apologize to Bromhall.

Bad Medicine

BIORHYTHMS

Biorhythms seem to have originated in 1887 by Wilhelm Fliess, a German physician. They were introduced into the United States around 1960 by George S. Thommen, a Swiss importer. Biorhythms are not the same as biological rhythms, which are valid biological cycles.

Biorhythms Predict Every Waking Moment!

Fliess claimed that every body cell has a cycle that plays an important role in the peaks and valleys in an individual's vitality and mental and physical strengths. He believed that these cycles, or biorhythms, even determined the date when a person would die.

Fliess also claimed that everyone is basically bisexual. Characteristics he labeled as "male"—such as strength, courage, and endurance—functioned in a twenty-three-day cycle. "Female" characteristics—such as sensitivity, intuition, and love—were keyed to a twenty-eight-day cycle (which was different from the menstrual cycle).

In the 1920s, an Austrian engineer by the name of Alfred Teltscher added a third cycle to Fliess's theory; biorhythms were expanded to include physical, intellectual, and emotional cycles. Since a person's birthdate determined when these cycles started, biorhythms were connected to astrology; sometime around 1900, Herman Swoboda added an astrological aspect to biorhythms.

An s-shaped curve. According to biorhythm theory, the physical cycle lasts twenty-three days, the emotional cycle lasts twenty-eight days,

THE NOSE KNOWS

Fliess's other "major" contribution to science was a theory that all illnesses were controlled by centers in the nose. The German physician believed that almost any condition could be treated by operating on the patient's nose.

BIO-CONFUSION

Bernard Gittelson was the most widely read popularizer of biorhythms. He tried to piggyback biorhythms onto the legitimate study of biological rhythms by deliberately combining the two concepts in his books. For example, Gittelson's book *Bio-Rhythm* contained the following sentence: "In man—the most complicated form of life—there are so many subtle, elaborate biological cycles that scientists have only begun to sketch in the nature of the larger cycles of human life that we call biorhythms." It's no wonder that the public was confused.

WHAT GOES AROUND, COMES AROUND

Biological rhythms are distinct from biorhythms. Many things in the living world display regular, cyclic behavior; most of these cycles are tied to the twenty-four-hour rotation period of the earth. The twenty-four-hour light and dark cycle or tidal cycle seem to be the "synchronizers" for these "circadian" rhythms (which are about twenty-four hours long). Some examples of these rhythms include activity cycles, feeding cycles, and sleeping cycles.

Biological rhythms differ in length from individual to individual. They develop slowly during the first one to two years of life, and vary somewhat in length within the same individual.

and the intellectual cycle lasts thirty-three days. All of these cycles start at "zero" at the moment of birth, and follow an "s-shaped" curve thereafter.

The emotional cycle reaches its peak in seven days, and crosses the zero line in another week. It then declines for a week to its minimum value, and rises again in another week. The cycle thus completes its curve within twenty-eight days.

Peak behavior and critical points. Biorhythm theory claims that when a cycle is above the zero line (positive), the abilities governed by it are increased, and vice versa. This means that a person can have one, two, or all three curves positive, negative, or mixed on any given day. A person is at the peak of his or her behavior when all three curves are at their positive maximum.

On the other hand, when all three curves are at their minimum, it is best not to leave home. When a cycle line is crossing the zero axis, it is said to be at its "critical" point; this is when people are most apt to be involved in a catastrophe in that particular area of life. Human disasters, according to the theory, are most likely to occur to a person who experiences more than one critical cycle on a given day.

An unscientific approach and disappearing research. Neither Thommen, who introduced biorhythms to the United States, nor Gittelson, who wrote *Bio-Rhythm*, is a scientist. Neither understands what valid scientific research involves. Instead, they have relied on the stories of people who have had tragedies in their lives that occurred on days when more than one of their cycles were critical or minimal. Gittelson has commented that "the most convincing studies of biorhythm are those you can do for yourself."

Fliess, Swoboda, and Teltscher all claimed to have conducted studies to validate biorhythm theory; however, none of these studies exists. Swoboda claimed that his eight trunks of research notes were lost when the Nazis invaded Vienna. Teltscher's research was never published. And Fliess's contributions consist of stories taken from psychiatric interviews with patients

Studies of Arnold Palmer's tournament victories were quoted to support biorhythm theory.

contained in rare books that were never translated from German into English.

The theory is tested with sports statistics. Nevertheless, several people attempted to test biorhythm theory by using published sports statistics. With an athlete's birthdate, someone could identify the athlete's biorhythm curves in order to compare them with his or her performance.

Studies that involved Arnold Palmer's golf tournament victories were quoted as support for the biorhythm theory. Supposedly, Palmer's physical curve would peak on the day of a "win," as long as the other two curves were not at the critical point.

After reexamining the data, skeptics discovered that incorrect statistical tests were applied to Palmer's victories. In truth, few of Palmer's wins were on days when his physical curve was high. Other studies of golfers' biorhythms failed to support the theory. In fact, the biorhythms of golfers on the dates they won tournaments showed results that did not differ from chance results. What's more, a study of the pitchers of no-hit baseball games arrived at similar results.

Nevertheless, biorhythm calculators and books continue to flourish. In spite of the unsound theory behind biorhythms and unsuccessful scientific attempts to prove the theory, some people continue to believe in—and others continue to profit from—the theory of biorhythms.

MUNCHAUSEN'S SYNDROME

Some people thrive on being admitted to the hospital—and even go so far as to have unnecessary surgery. These people are said to have "Munchausen's Syndrome," a disorder characterized by a chronic desire for unnecessary hospitalization or surgery.

WHAT'S IN A NAME?

Munchausen's Syndrome was named by R. Asher in a 1951 *Lancet* article. Although the condition has recently been renamed "Chronic Fictitious Illness," the old name remains popular.

Munchausen's Patients Crave Surgery and Hospital Care!

Munchausen's syndrome is named after the semi-fictional Baron Munchausen; although the Baron really lived, the book of his supposed adventures is a work of fiction. The fictional Munchausen was famous for lying dramatically about his adventures. Similarly, those who suffer from the syndrome named for him are famous for lying—in a dramatic way—about their medical condition.

People who have Munchausen's Syndrome tend to be socially isolated, with no close family ties or friends. They often arrive at the hospital emergency room with what appear to be genuine emergency symptoms, and many have scars that indicate previous surgeries. Munchausen's patients usually leave the hospital early—against medical advice—and without paying their bills.

A familiar pattern. Munchausen's Syndrome is rather rare: Through 1990, there were about 200 known cases of the condition. Many patients are repeatedly admitted to the hospital—some as often as 100 times.

Author Loren Pankratz noted that these admissions often followed a pattern. Patients usually use the same symptoms from one hospitalization to the next, adding a minor symptom each time. Since they are usually familiar with medical terminology and hospital procedures, they are able to present a convincing case. Many Munchausen's patients are also drug

BARON MUNCHAUSEN's
NARRATIVE
OF HIS
MARVELLOUS TRAVELS
AND
CAMPAIGNS
IN
RUSSIA.

HUMBLY DEDICATED AND RECOMMENDED
TO
COUNTRY GENTLEMEN;

AND, IF THEY PLEASE,

TO BE REPEATED AS THEIR OWN, AFTER A HUNT
AT HORSE RACES, IN WATERING-PLACES, AND
OTHER SUCH POLITE ASSEMBLIES; ROUND THE
BOTTLE AND FIRE-SIDE.

OXFORD:

Printed for the EDITOR, and fold by the Bookfellers there and
at Cambridge, alfo in London by the Bookfellers of Picca-
dilly, the Royal Exchange, and M. SMITH, at No. 46, in
Fleet-ftreet.—And in Dublin by P. BYRNE, No. 108, Graf-
ton-ftreet.

MDCCLXXXVI.

First edition title page of Baron Munchausen's travel book.

abusers who deceive physicians in order to obtain prescription drugs.

Medical problems real and imagined. Many Munchausen patients do have some underlying medical problems. Others have faked their conditions by mixing blood into their urine specimens, by producing fevers through injections, and even by injuring themselves, incurring serious cuts and broken bones.

Recently there have been reports of "Munchausen's Syndrome by Proxy"—in which a parent hurts his or her children in order to get attention, often from medical personnel. The children involved are often infants or toddlers who are too young to tell of their own symptoms or lack of symptoms.

What motivates a patient to behave this way is unclear. Surgical addiction, lack of money, and a tendency toward self-mutilation may all play a role in Munchausen's Syndrome. Munchausen's patients may also enjoy receiving pity in place of love, but guilt often prevents them from accepting the pity.

POPULAR PSYCHIC SURGEONS

Psychic surgery is most popular in Brazil and the Philippines, where it is a multi-million dollar a year industry. The best known psychic surgeons—"Arigo," whose real name was José Pedro de Freitas, and Antonio Agpaoa, of the Philippines— treated several hundred people between them.

PSYCHIC SURGERY

Psychic surgeons supposedly perform "surgery" that heals instantly and leaves no scar. After rubbing the part of the body that is said to be diseased, the "surgeon" reaches through the patient's skin with bare hands to remove tissue that is believed to be tumorous. The patient, seemingly cured, is then sent home considerably poorer.

Psychic Surgeons Work Miracles Without Scalpels and Knives!

Blood *seems* to flow as the psychic surgeon appears to remove tissue without the use of a scalpel. Trained magicians, however, have seen through the so-called surgeons' bogus operations. By observing the actual "operation" and films of the operation, magicians have discovered that the entire procedure is actually sleight of hand.

Magician James Randi perfected his own performance of psychic surgery to such an extent that he can't be distinguished from the psychic surgeons themselves. Randi—unlike the other psychic surgeons— admits that it is all a trick and he has revealed how it is done.

False fingers and cow's blood. The secret of psychic surgery lies in careful advance preparation. A false "thumb tip"—a standard item at magic supply houses—is essential. This rubber false finger, bigger and longer than a person's own thumb, fits over the real thumb. Inside the hollow thumb tip, a number of "props" can be stored, such as animal tissue; chicken, pig, or cow blood; chicken fat; and sinew (tendons). With the tissue and blood inside the hollow thumb, the surgeon can slip on the thumb tip when he or she picks up gauze bandages for cleansing.

The surgeon can then squeeze the thumb tip for a flow of blood. With the tip removed to the inside of one hand, tissue can be squeezed out of the open end of the thumb tip.

When working on a heavy person's abdomen, the psychic surgeon can actually appear to place his or her hands inside the patient's body with the aid of some clever finger bending. At the end of the operation, the surgeon disposes of the thumb tip with the soiled and bloody gauze from the "operation."

A costly operation. Practice makes the psychic surgeon's movements very difficult to detect—at least for those who are not trained in magic and sleight of hand. However unlikely it may seem, people are fooled. Some have refused to see a regular physician to treat a real tumor until it is so advanced that it is no longer operable. In fact, a follow-up investigation of some of the people who were treated by psychic surgeons revealed that almost all of the patients died within a year or two of their visit to the phoney physicians.

Intergalactic Inventions

ANTI-GRAVITY DEVICES

One of the fondest dreams of many inventors has been to find a device that can neutralize gravity; such a dream seems to be theoretically impossible. Although scientists do not fully understand gravity, they do know that it is not a bipolar force. In other words, while magnets have a north and south pole—with like poles repelling and opposite poles attracting—gravity apparently exerts force in only one direction.

Device Harnesses the Forces of Gravity!

The "Dean Drive," invented by Norman Dean of Washington, D.C., in the 1950s, is basically an "anchorless winch": It converts rotating motion into motion that is directed in one direction. Dean's device received a U.S. patent, and a number of engineers actually believed that the Dean Drive could be developed into a useful machine.

GRAVITY ALWAYS WINS

It is unlikely that any anti-gravitational force can exist, except of course for something like a rocket exhaust thrusting against gravity. What has eluded inventors is a reactionless thrust against gravity. Merely canceling gravity would not provide any propulsive force to push against the earth; that means that a "gravity shield" would be of limited use. This hasn't stopped inventors from producing devices that they claim to be anti-gravity inventions or gravity shields.

Others have analyzed the tiny amount of thrust generated by the device. They have concluded that the force is present because static friction in one direction is less than it is in the opposite direction. In other words, something cannot be gotten for nothing, and gravity is not really being canceled out.

Not everyone agreed with this diagnosis of the Dean Drive, but since the 1960s, nothing further has been heard about Norman Dean's anti-gravitational device. Some say that it didn't really work as advertised. In any case, no other anti-gravity device has ever obtained a U.S. patent.

THE DEATH RAY

In 1924, electrical genius Nikola Tesla supposedly claimed that he invented a death ray that was capable of stopping an airplane in mid-flight. Nothing more came to light until 1934, when Tesla was quoted as saying that his ray worked on an entirely new principle of physics.

Astonishing Death Ray Stops Airplanes in Mid-Flight!

Tesla claimed that his amazing death ray was capable of destroying 10,000 planes from a distance of 250 miles. Each ray would require the construction of a $2 million plant, located at a high, strategic point. A network of twelve such death ray plants, Tesla claimed, would protect the United States from aerial invasion.

Electrical genius Nikola Tesla.

LASER'S FOREBEAR?

Nikola Tesla's death ray has been called the grandfather of the laser, which was first put on the market in 1960. Such a relationship is, in a word, doubtful.

Two years later, Tesla was still trying to sell his death ray to an uninterested public; the military, too, was strangely uninterested. In the end, Tesla's invention never got off the ground, and no papers on the death ray were found after the inventor died in 1943.

FLIGHT HOAXES

The Wright brothers' flight in 1903 at Kitty Hawk, North Carolina, was the first successful airplane flight. A number of previous flight attempts, however, never got off the ground. Not all were hoaxes, while others became hoaxes after the fact.

Artificial Wings Carry Birdmen to Awesome New Heights!

One of the earliest "birdmen" was Eilmer of Malmsbury, who strapped on wings sometime around the year 1010. The early aviator supposedly flew more than 607 feet—a "stadium" in Roman measure—before crashing and breaking his legs.

In 1066 William of Malmsbury described Eilmer's feat in his *De Gestis regum Anglorum*. That leaves approximately a forty-five year gap between the event and the time it was first recorded—plenty of time to exaggerate the length of Eilmer's eleventh-century flight. Although there may not have been any conscious deception at the time, the flight of the birdman of Malmsbury is a bit too far flung to be believable.

A birdman. Although the artist and inventor Leonardo da Vinci designed ornithopters, parachutes, and helicopters, he apparently never used them himself. Giovanni Battista Danti (c.1477-1517)—the other major "birdman" of the period before 1600—reportedly made several flights.

Danti's main flight—which supposedly took place in Perugia, Italy, in 1498 or 1499—was described in *Elogia Civicum Perusinorum*, written by Caesar Alesi in 1652. Danti made the wings that he wore, perfecting his technique in flights over Lake Trasimeno. During his main flight, Danti flew across the public square, where a great crowd was gathered for a wedding. When one of the iron struts that controlled the left wing broke, Danti was thrown onto the roof of St. Mary's Church, injuring his leg. The written version of these "facts" did not appear until 150 years after the event, and the total distance Danti covered in his flight was not stated; it seems, however, that reports of Danti's flight have been greatly exaggerated.

GASOLINE ADDITIVES

Many so-called inventors have claimed to have created an automobile engine that runs on water; others claim to have discovered some sort of additive that can be mixed with gasoline to fuel an automobile engine that gets hundreds of miles per gallon. The search for inexpensive fuel has led to more than a few schemes to profit from undelivered promises.

Miracle Gas from Neptune Gets Astronomical Gas Mileage!

In 1917, John Andrews demonstrated a mysterious green powder to the U.S. Navy; the powder, when mixed with water, made a fuel that ran a gasoline engine. Suspecting that they had been tricked, however, navy personnel did not follow up on the amazing gasoline powder.

Andrews produced no more inventions until 1935, when he again demonstrated the powder for the Bureau of Standards. Nothing came of the demonstration. Even so, Andrews was murdered in 1937, and the powder and his papers were stolen from his Pennsylvania home.

Secret powder and spacemen from Neptune. In 1973, Guido Franch of Chicago, Illinois, demonstrated a similar powder to automobile companies and others. Even though the powder was not available for analysis, Franch demanded millions of dollars in exchange for his invention; apparently put off by the $10-million tab, investors did not clamber to purchase Franch's secret powder.

Franch claimed that he did not make the powder, but had gotten the idea—and perhaps a supply of the powder—from a German chemist

---

WHY HUMANS DON'T FLY

The theme of man flying by using wings is common in mythology and in literature. In truth, however, all attempts to fly using movable, strapped-on wings have led to immediate—and often fatal—plunges to the ground.

Anatomists and physiologists have pointed out that the human body is too heavy to be lifted by human arm and chest muscles, no matter how large or well-designed the set of bird-like wings is. Flying birds have hollow bones, organs that minimize weight (such as air sacs instead of lungs, and only one ovary instead of two), and never weigh more than thirty-five pounds.

A PRICEY LIGHTER FLUID

In exchange for his miraculous gasoline additive, Guido Franch wanted a little financial security. To be exact, he wanted $250,000 up front, with $10 million put into an escrow account that became his as soon as he revealed the secret of producing the powder. On top of that, he wanted one cent per gallon of fuel made. No one agreed to Franch's terms, and an analysis of the fuel showed that it was nothing but a substance similar to lighter fluid.

named Kraft. It seems Franch knew Kraft's mistress, who had been given a supply of the powder. He also believed that John Andrews—whom he claimed not to know—had been given some of the powder. Finally, when pressured for more answers about the gasoline additive, Franch revealed one more bit of secret information: The miracle powder, he said, came from the "Black Eagles," a group of spacemen from the planet Neptune.

Heroes,
Bad Guys, and
Impostors

Presidential Hoaxes

ABRAHAM LINCOLN HOAXES

Abraham Lincoln, who was in office from 1861 to 1865, has been indirectly involved in a number of hoaxes—after he was assassinated in 1865. His signature and documents have been widely forged, and words that he never spoke have been written into history through phoney speeches and quotes.

History Put Words in President Lincoln's Mouth!

The Bixby letter was supposedly written by Lincoln to a widow who lost five sons in the Civil War. However, experts say that Lincoln did not actually write the letter, the original of which has never been found. The president's secretary, John Hay—an expert in imitating Lincoln's handwriting—probably wrote the letter to the grieving mother. What's more, it seems that the writer of the letter was mistaken about how many sons Bixby had lost: Bixby lost *two*—not *five*—sons in the Civil War.

In 1928 and 1929, the *Atlantic Monthly* magazine mistakenly published a collection of phoney Lincoln papers when it printed love letters that Lincoln supposedly wrote to Ann Rutledge. Reading between the lines, Lincoln scholars dismissed the letters as fakes, and the magazine discontinued publishing the phoney presidential love notes.

Words the president never spoke. During the 1880s, a number of Lincoln speeches were published—speeches that contained material

This was the last picture ever taken of Abraham Lincoln. The glass negative cracked during developing, and the photographer never got a second chance to pose the president. Honest Abe was assassinated the following week.

never written or even uttered by President Lincoln. For instance, he supposedly said:

> I see in the near future a crisis that unnerves me, and causes me to tremble for the safety of my country. As a result of war, corporations have been enthroned and an era of corruption in high places will follow, and the money power of the country will endeavor to prolong its reign by working upon the prejudices of the people until all the wealth is aggregated in a few hands and the republic is destroyed.

The trouble is, Lincoln never said this. Other made-up quotes have been used to suggest that Lincoln favored a high tariff and that he favored Italian unification, an issue he never actually addressed.

In 1896, *McClure's Magazine* published what it called "Lincoln's Lost Speech." Since no one had written down the speech, which was supposedly delivered at the Republican State Convention in Bloomington, Illinois, in 1856, experts believed that the original text had been lost. In 1930, after carefully studying the speech that appeared in *McClure's*, Lincoln scholars concluded that it was a fake. The original text of "Lincoln's Lost Speech" has never been found.

Plagued by prankster Dick Tuck, Richard Nixon's sense of humor was put to the test.

DICK TUCK'S HOAXES

Dick Tuck pulled off a number of hoaxes in the realm of politics, but he is best known for his pranks on Richard Nixon. Some were hoaxes, others were simply pranks, but all were at the expense of the thirty-seventh president of the United States.

Political Prankster Preys on "Tricky Dick" Nixon!

Charged with setting up a college rally to introduce Nixon, Tuck obtained a 4,000-seat auditorium. He knew, however, that only a small group would attend; a total of *forty* people entered the 4,000-seat auditorium. Before Nixon began, Tuck announced that he was going to wait for more people to show up. None did; instead, ten people left.

Attempting to stall the proceedings, Tuck asked Nixon all sorts of questions—under the guise of "introducing" the politician. Finally, he said "Richard Nixon will now speak on the World Monetary Fund." Nixon, who had never intended to speak on the World Monetary Fund, was at first stunned and speechless.

Garbage trucks and a kiss on the cheek. When Nixon was running with Dwight D. Eisenhower for reelection as vice president, the Republican Convention was held in San Francisco. Tuck discovered that the main route taken by many garbage trucks going to the city dump passed right by the convention center. This inspired him to use the dump trucks to advertise his opinion of the vice president: Tuck had posters applied to each garbage truck that proclaimed "Dump Nixon."

Heroes, Bad Guys, and Impostors

During the 1960 Nixon/Kennedy race, Tuck orchestrated yet another incident. As Nixon descended from an airplane the day after his first debate with John F. Kennedy, a woman—sent by Tuck—approached him. She kissed Nixon on the cheek and said, "That's all right, Mr. Nixon. He beat you last night, but you'll win next time." A bit unsettled, Nixon eventually managed to compose himself.

AN ACTION-PACKED SPEECH

Dick Tuck denies having authored the hoax that most people think was his best ever—although he claims he wishes he had masterminded the prank. As the story goes, Richard Nixon was delivering a speech from the rear platform of a train. Someone dressed in a conductor's uniform motioned at the train, which left the station—while Nixon was **still talking.** Tuck denies having had anything to do with the incident. In fact, the prank is not documented, and actually may never have happened.

Bad Guy Hoaxes

HITLER SURVIVED WORLD WAR II

As the Russians advanced within Berlin, Germany, on April 30, 1945, Germany's führer (leader) Adolf Hitler was in his bunker under the Reich's Chancellery. He was in poor health: his hands trembled severely, possibly because of Parkinson's disease, possibly because he chronically abused amphetamines. After the Russians overran Berlin, the Kremlin announced Hitler's death on May 2; some thought the Russians had ulterior motives in proclaiming Hitler dead.

Adolf Hitler Is Alive and Well!

In its May 2 announcement, Tass, a Russian news service, stated that the Germans had reported that Hitler had died at noon the previous day, and he had named Admiral Doenitz to succeed him as chancellor. The Tass statement added that "by spreading the news of Hitler's death, the German Fascists apparently wish to give Hitler the means of leaving the stage and going underground." Stories of Hitler's escape spread like wildfire. Some said that he and Nazi officer Bormann had escaped from Germany by taking a submarine to South America; others said Hitler was alive and well and living in Antarctica.

Bodies in the garden. The Russians delayed releasing the autopsy report on Hitler's body for more than twenty years—which only fanned the fire of rumors about Hitler's escape. The report did not surface until

HITLER'S BUNKER

Although the world will probably never know exactly what happened on April 30, 1945, some things are clear. Hitler was not alone in his bunker under the Reich's Chancellery in Berlin. Among those present were:

- Nazis Joseph Goebbels and Martin Bormann
- Eva Braun, Hitler's mistress
- two of Hitler's secretaries
- Hitler's chauffeur Erich Kampka
- Hitler's servant Heinz Linge
- several guards

Heroes, Bad Guys, and Impostors

1968, when it appeared—buried—in a Russian book by a former Soviet intelligence officer by the name of Lev Bezymensky. The book claimed that Russian counterintelligence (SMERSH) had captured the guard who witnessed the bodies of Hitler and Eva Braun being taken from the bunker to the garden and burned. SMERSH discovered the bodies of Joseph Goebbels and his wife, and, on May 4, 1945, dug up the bodies of a male and female who had been buried in the garden outside of the bunker.

At first, the agents did not believe that the remains were the bodies of Hitler and Eva Braun, but a careful search of the bunker did not produce their bodies. When the guard who witnessed the burning later added that he was present when the burned bodies were placed in a bomb crater and covered with dirt, SMERSH carefully examined the exhumed bodies.

The autopsy report: The teeth tell all. The autopsy report of the two bodies buried in the garden said that both died by biting into a

Soldiers give the Nazi salute to (from left to right) Joseph Goebbels, Adolf Hitler, and Rudolf Hess. Goebbels was among the Nazis who perished in Hitler's bunker.

poison capsule (cyanide): Glass fragments had been found in the mouths of both corpses. The male body had also been shot in the head—after he had taken the poison. And, like Hitler, the man had only one testicle.

Dental records provided positive proof that the body in the garden was that of the infamous Nazi leader. Using the remains of the body's extensive dental work, the Soviets matched Hitler's teeth with records from his dentist's office. Eva Braun's body, too, was identified by her dental work.

Dead men don't travel. Reporters hoped to question Bezymensky about his book, but the Soviets allowed no such meeting. The Soviets also claimed that Hitler had requested Heinz Linge, his servant, to shoot him after he swallowed the poison capsule, but Linge denied having shot Hitler. In fact, Linge and another witness both claimed that Hitler had not taken poison, but had shot himself.

Clearly, Hitler did not escape. But that hasn't stopped people from claiming to have "sighted" him in nearly every country of the world since the end of World War II. What's more—putting aside the question of whether or not Hitler died in his bunker—he would now be well over 100 years old if he were still alive.

JACK THE RIPPER HOAXES

At least five women died at the hands of a single murderer in London in 1888; the killer, however, was never publicly identified and may never have been caught. Over the years, a number of books and articles have claimed to solve the killings and reveal the identity of the killer. The murders, committed by a man known as Jack the Ripper, were no hoax; but the quest to find out *who* he was and *why* he savagely murdered his victims has inspired more than a few wild stories.

Five Women Die Gruesome Deaths at Hands of Ripper—Whoever He Was!

Although some people attribute eighteen murders to the Ripper, only five can be definitely attributed to the same killer. The first killing

The London killer might have called himself "Jack the Ripper," but the name itself may be a hoax.

was that of forty-three-year-old Mary Ann Nichols, on August 31, 1888. The body was found on Buck's Row (now Durward Street) in Whitechapel, then a dangerous slum area of London's East End. As a matter of fact, Whitechapel was where all the murders took place. Nichols, a prostitute, had her throat cut, as did all the victims; there were also several deep slashes in the abdomen.

·25. Sept· 1888.

Dear Boss,

I keep on hearing the police have caught me but they wont fix me just yet. I have laughed when they look so clever and talk about being on the right track. That joke about Leather apron gave me real fits. I am down on whores and I shant quit ripping them till I do get buckled. Grand work the last job was. I gave the lady no time to squeal. How can they catch me. I love my work and want to start again. you will soon hear of me with my funny little games. I saved some of the proper red stuff in a ginger beer bottle over the last job to write with but it went thick like glue and I cant use it. Red ink is fit enough I hope ha. ha. The next job I do I shall clip the ladys ears off and send to the police officers just for jolly wouldnt you. Keep this letter back till I do a bit more work. then give it out straight. My knife's so nice and sharp I want to get to work right away if I get a chance. Good luck.

yours truly
Jack the Ripper

Dont mind me giving the trade name

Annie Chapman, the second victim, a forty-seven-year-old prostitute, was found murdered on September 8, on Hanbury Street. Chapman's body had been terribly mutilated: Her intestines had been strewn about and her uterus had been removed. On September 30, the third victim, prostitute Elizabeth Stride ('Long Liz') was discovered with her throat cut, although her body was otherwise unmutilated; the authorities believed that her killer was interrupted before he could mutilate her. Catharine Eddowes ("Katie Kelly"), age forty-six, was also killed that night in Mitre Square; she, too, was a prostitute. Eddowes was severely mutilated and cut about the face; her uterus and one kidney were removed.

By this time, the news agencies and police had received several infamous letters signed "Jack the Ripper." The writer of the letters boasted that he would not be caught and that, after cutting off the ears of one of his victims, he would send them to the police. A later letter enclosed a piece of human kidney, although it can't be determined whether it was the one removed from Eddowes.

The final and most horrific murder occurred inside the room where prostitute Mary Jane Kelly lived. On November 9, the body of Kelly, who was about 25, was found in her bed. The body was terribly mutilated. This was to be Jack the Ripper's last killing. Some people believe that the killer suddenly died; others believe he was secretly captured and committed to an insane asylum; and still others speculate that the Ripper quit after he had eliminated all of his intended victims.

The queen, a baby girl, and black mail. Author Stephen Knight proposed a "solution" to the murders, but he had no facts to bolster his theory. In fact, his main witness admitted that his story was pure fiction. Knight believed that all five of the victims knew each other. They were specific targets of the killer, who was trying to dispose of them because they were blackmailing the queen.

According to Knight's story, Queen Victoria's grandson, Prince Edward Albert, who was second in line for the throne, secretly married a Catholic girl and had a baby girl with her. This child, who would be third in line for the throne, was a Catholic (by birth) and would have destroyed the entire Anglican basis of the monarchy if she ever became

---

THE LONG LIST OF SUSPECTS

Many men have been named as the infamous Jack the Ripper over the past century. They include:

- Druitt, a mentally ill barrister
- Gull, a royal physician
- "Leather Apron"—possibly John Pizer—a butcher
- Stephenson, a mad poet
- Stanley, the father of a man who caught syphilis from a prostitute
- Pedachenko or Ostrog, a Russian physician
- Eddy, the Duke of Clarence, a royal grandson
- Cream, a mentally ill surgeon, and
- Kosminski, a man who despised prostitutes

A portrait of a Ripper?
Sir William Gull.

queen. The Home Secretary, therefore, issued the order to kidnap the woman and kill the child.

Supposedly, the five murdered women had witnessed the kidnapping and were attempting to blackmail the queen. According to Knight's theory, three men acted as the murderers: Sir William Gull, the Queen's physician; John Netley, the Queen's coachman; and Robert Anderson, an assistant commissioner of the Metropolitan Police. It would have been easy to lure a prostitute into a royal coach by rolling down a window and extending a hand with a gold coin in it. Since the murders were committed inside a royal coach, there were no witnesses. The bodies, in turn, were dumped in an alley.

Heroes, Bad Guys, and Impostors

Gull committed the murders, making them look like the work of a madman who was seeking revenge for a personal betrayal. What's more, Gull's involvement ties in a chalk inscription that was found on a wall near one of the killings. The inscription—"The Juwes are the men that will not be blamed for nothing"—had previously been taken as an illiterate reference to "Jews"; Knight, however, notes that "the Juwes" referred to a high Masonic official, known to the upper ranks of Freemasonry (a fraternal organization). As it turns out, Gull was a Freemason.

This story, supposedly told to Knight by the son of artist Walter Sickert, has a lot going for it. But it doesn't hold up under close investigation. For instance, there were two laws that prevented the throne of England from ever being occupied by a Catholic. According to The Royal Marriages Act, any secret marriage of the royal family could be set aside as invalid if the royal family member was under the age of twenty-five or had married without the queen's consent; Eddy, not yet in his mid-twenties, had definitely tied the knot without grand-mama's official blessing. And the Act of Settlement of 1700 minces no words in excluding any person who married a Roman Catholic from inheriting the crown. Between these two laws, the motivation for the entire plot crumbles. In any case, Walter Sickert's son Joseph admitted that the whole story was a fraud.

Visions of murder. Robert J. Lees (1848-1931), a spiritual medium, offered another hoax to explain the Jack the Ripper murders. On April 28, 1895, the Chicago *Sunday Times and Herald* ran a story claiming that Lees had a vision of one of the killings before it occurred. Lees apparently had approached the police, but they quickly dismissed him as a quack. The following night, however, a murder occurred exactly where, when, and how Lees had described it; the police were suddenly more interested in what the psychic had to say.

The next time Lees went to the police with another vision, he told them that the killer would cut off the ears of his victim. The police were particularly interested since they had just received the letter—signed "Jack the Ripper." Lees supposedly accompanied the police to the scene of the next Ripper killing and received an impression of the killer that allowed him to trace the murderer back to his house.

The home was that of a prominent physician; although the physician has not been named, Gull, once again, is regarded as the suspect.

THE LAST ATTACK

The Ripper's final victim, Mary Jane Kelly was killed indoors. According to Stephen Knight's scenario, another Mary Kelly (also known as Katie Kelly) was accidentally killed when she was mistaken for Mary Jane Kelly. When the killer or killers realized their mistake, they tracked down Mary Jane Kelly and killed her at home. With her death, all of the queen's blackmailers were dead.

After a bit of cajoling, the doctor's wife agreed to speak to the police; what she told them didn't paint a flattering picture of her husband. The doctor, it seems, had a strange character flaw that caused him to fly into rages and sometimes to behave sadistically. Judged before a panel of his peers, he was declared insane and committed to an asylum, where he died shortly thereafter.

Lees's story, too, has a number of problems. To begin with, the police deny that any of this happened—and their files don't indicate otherwise. Furthermore, Gull was neither judged insane nor committed; in fact, a thorough search failed to find such records for any London physician who had been committed to an asylum. Apparently, Edwin T. Woodhall, a British journalist, was responsible for spreading this Ripper tale. Woodhall reworked the original 1895 Chicago newspaper article in the 1930s, and, accepted as true, the article was eventually reprinted in many books and magazines.

The Ripper remains anonymous. Many other suspects have been identified as Jack the Ripper, but it is unlikely that the bloody truth will ever come to light. Many people hoped that the London files—sealed for a century—would offer the final solution. Once opened, however, the files simply listed the usual suspects, with no real proof to identify the killer.

QADAFFI CAUGHT OFF GUARD

Libyan leader Muammar Qadaffi had a tendency to do away with his rivals. It was therefore no surprise when, in November 1984, word got out that Abdul Hamid Bakkush, the Prime Minister Qadaffi overthrew in 1969, was on the Qadaffi's hit list. The Egyptian government decided to protect Bakkush—who was living in Cairo in 1984—by faking his assassination.

Libyan Leader Fooled by Fake Photo!

The Egyptians made photographs of Bakkush—who appeared to be dead—covered with blood and lying in a pool of blood. After receiving the photos from Egyptian intelligence agents, Libya announced publicly that Bakkush had been killed by Libyan "suicide squads." The

Libyan leader
Muammar El Qaddafi.

following day, Egypt announced that it had hoaxed Libya: Bakkush was still alive. They also announced that four members of the Libyan assassination team were under arrest. As it turns out, the team's two Britons and two Maltese members had hired Egyptian collaborators who were in fact undercover agents.

Fake I.D.'s

FERDINAND WALDO DEMARA

Ferdinand Waldo Demara (1922-1982) has been called "The Great Impostor"—and rightfully so. He has successfully impersonated many individuals including a surgeon, psychologist, college dean, dentist, professor, and a Trappist monk.

Impostor Bamboozles Surgeons, Monks, and Navy Brass!

Demara grew up in Lawrence, Massachusetts. Running away from home at the age of sixteen, he joined a Trappist monastery, where—put off by the strict atmosphere—he stayed for only two years. Demara then enlisted in the U.S. Army, and, assigned to Kessler Field in Biloxi, Mississippi, he realized almost immediately that he had made a mistake.

Demara discovered that the orderlies who rounded up recruits for transfer to other units seemed to avoid the worst duties. Soon, he masqueraded as an orderly, complete with fake armband and clipboard; what's more, he seemed to know exactly what he was doing. In short, Demara had taken his first step toward a life as an impostor.

Twice Trappist (see box) and the art of teaching science. Having assumed the identity of his fellow soldier, Demara was admitted to another monastery. All went well—for a while—until a student from the first monastery recognized Demara from his former monastery. After only one week, Demara fled, eventually enlisting in the U.S. Navy. Just

Heroes, Bad Guys, and Impostors

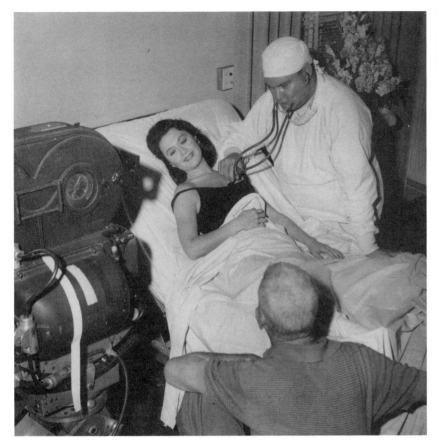

The great impostor, Fred Demara, playing doctor in *The Hypnotic Eye*, a United Artists movie.

after the bombing of Pearl Harbor, he was sent to Hospital School, where he received first aid training.

Demara, now interested in the medical field, applied for advanced training. When he was turned down on the grounds that he did not have enough education, he managed to obtain the credentials of one Dr. Robert Linton French, a psychologist. Using French's credentials, Demara secured a teaching position in science at a boy's school run by a Catholic order. Staying just one lesson ahead of his pupils, Demara managed to keep his scam afloat until the abbot checked his credentials. Fired, he stole the abbot's car and headed for Chicago.

Fake papers, a war crime and eighteen months in the slammer. Once in Chicago, Demara started training for the priesthood, but he left when it looked like he'd have to go through another rigorous training period that included self-denial. Using his psychology "credentials," Demara became dean of the School of Philosophy at Gannon College in

Erie, Pennsylvania. But his grand schemes for improving the college—and his position there—soon led to his dismissal.

Demara then traveled to an abbey in Washington, where he successfully ran a student psychological counseling center. Appointed as deputy sheriff, Demara was again undone by a background check that turned up his criminal past. Arrested and led away in handcuffs, Demara was charged with deserting the navy in wartime, a capital crime. In spite of his memorable self-defense, the Great Impostor served eighteen months in prison.

A growing academic career. Freed from prison, Demara immediately enrolled as a law student in Boston. After completing his first year of law school he left for Maine, where he became a biology professor at a small college. After helping to turn the small college into a university, he left in a fit of anger when he was informed that he would not be promoted at the new university. But he didn't leave empty-handed; before quitting those hallowed halls, Demara managed to procure copies of the credentials of Joseph Cyr, the physician who treated some of the faculty (see box).

Fifteen minutes of fame ... and then some. Having sold his life story to *Life* magazine, Demara committed a $2,500 mistake. The general public, now familiar with Demara's face and checkered background, was no longer easily duped. Appointed as a prison officer under the name Ben W. Jones, Demara soon became warden of the maximum security block at the Huntsville, Texas, jail. When a prisoner saw the article in *Life*, Demara's prison career came to an abrupt end.

Returning to Maine, Demara ran a local school—until he was arrested yet again. When the local townspeople rallied to his defense, praising his abilities as a teacher, the charges were dropped and Demara left town.

The end of his brilliant career. Demara's career as an impostor suffered a final blow when Robert Crichton's book *The Great Impostor* appeared in 1959. It became all but impossible to continue the masquerade, and Demara was forced to get by on his own name.

Heroes, Bad Guys, and Impostors

After moving to California, he worked in various youth counseling positions. Twice charged with child molestation, he was successfully defended by attorney Melvin Belli. Demara worked in his final position—as a visiting counselor at Good Samaritan Hospital in Anaheim, California—until illness forced him to retire. Demara died at the age of sixty on June 8, 1982.

MARTIN GUERRE

The case of Martin Guerre (born in 1525) is one of the most famous and complex cases of imposture. The basic story is simple. A woman named Bertrande de Rols Guerre and her husband Martin Guerre lived in the village of Artigat in southern France. In 1553, after nearly ten years of marriage, Martin Guerre disappeared.

French Impostor Sentenced to Hang!

Four years later, a man claiming to be Monsieur Guerre appeared in the village. He looked something like Martin and he knew a lot about Bertrande—and about Martin's past life. If he wasn't the real Martin Guerre, he had studied his subject well. Bertrande accepted him as her husband, and within the three years they lived together, they had two children. Many people accepted this man as the real Martin, and when others expressed their doubts to Bertrande, she reassured them that he was, indeed, the real Martin Guerre.

Curiosity kills the impostor. When Martin began asking his wife's relatives about how much property she owned and what it was worth, he aroused more than a little suspicion; her relatives informed the authorities that something was amiss. The new Guerre (whose real name was Arnaud du Tilh) was arrested and brought to trial for adultery and imposture. Convicted, du Tilh was sentenced to death by hanging—

although he insisted to the bitter end that he was Bertrande's legitimate husband.

During the trial, the long-absent *original* Martin Guerre returned to the village. Having lost a leg in battle, he was nonetheless easily recognized—and accepted—by Bertrande, her family, and the rest of the villagers. The court, although suspicious of the war veteran for having deserted his family, decided not to prosecute him.

A possible accomplice. The court also had to decide whether Bertrande was consciously aware of du Tilh's deception and whether she had willingly participated in adultery. After a lengthy deliberation, the judges decided that Bertrande had, indeed, been deceived—for more than three years—by a man who pretended to be her husband. Still, the court's reasoning seemed more like a pardon than a verdict of innocence. In fact, the court ordered Bertrande to pardon her husband and to reconcile with him since she had been so easily led into fraud by the bogus Martin Guerre.

MARTIN GUERRE AND *SOMMERSBY*

The French movie *Le Retour de Martin Guerre* (1981) (*The Return of Martin Guerre*) is based on this case. Although the film is basically accurate, some historians continue to dispute certain aspects of the case—for example, whether Martin's wife, Bertrande, was involved in the ruse. The movie *Sommersby* (1993), starring Richard Gere and Jody Foster, is a remake of *Le Retour*. The plots are very similar, except in Sommersby, the hoax takes place just after the Civil War.

Outlaw Impostors

JESSE JAMES

Even though a coroner positively identified the corpse of Jesse James (1847-1882), many people believed that the Missouri bank robber was alive and growing old gracefully. The identified corpse, however, was a ringer for Jesse James: Like the outlaw, it had two scars on the right side of the chest, and the tip of the middle finger of the left hand was missing.

Bad Guys Don't Die!

Scarcely one year after James was supposed to have died, a Missouri farmer claimed to have seen him alive. Soon, a number of men came forward, each of whom claimed to be the one-and-only legendary pistol-packer: At least seventeen impostors claimed to be the real Jesse James. Such claims were especially popular during the late 1920s and 1930s, when James impostors toured in traveling tent shows.

A sudden identity crisis. Kentucky writer Joe Creason claims that one absent-minded James pretender showed up in a Kentucky town—where the James gang had once pulled off a bank robbery. When the U.S. Marshall asked if he was Jesse James, he said he was. The marshall then pulled an old, yellowed document from his pocket; "In that case," he said, "I have here a warrant for your arrest, charging you with the robbery of the Bank of Columbia and the murder of the cashier." The self-professed outlaw grew a little pale. "However," the marshall continued, "on the off chance that you just might not be Jesse James, I'm giving you ten minutes to get out of town." Fleeing, the impostor replied, "Marshall, I can beat that time with five minutes to spare!"

The last man to claim that he was Jesse James was J. Frank Dalton. Before dying in 1951, he managed to convince many people that he was the infamous outlaw—even though his story was inconsistent and inaccurate, and his handwriting was not like James's.

Rebel without a cause—
Billy the Kid.

Billie the Kid, a copy from
a very old tin-type.

BRUSHY BILL AND BILLY THE KID

A number of impostors claimed that the notorious outlaw Billy didn't die as a kid; among them was a Texan by the name of Ollie L. "Brushy Bill" Roberts.

Orlando Scott—a Chicago, Illinois, doctor—stands with the mummy that toured sideshows as the body of John Wilkes Booth.

Heroes, Bad Guys, and Impostors

Billy the Kid Grows Up!

Supposedly, the twenty-two-year-old Kid—whose real name was William Bonney—escaped the trap set for him by Sheriff Pat Garrett at Fort Sumner, New Mexico, and lived to a ripe old age as "Brushy Bill." Skeptics pointed out, however, that Roberts had also claimed to be Frank James (the brother of Jesse James). Using authenticated photographs of the Kid and "Brushy Bill" to compare twenty-five facial "landmarks," experts determined, by computer analysis, that the two men were clearly different individuals. As author Gregory Byrne has said, "It seems bad guys, or at least their legends, don't want to die."

JOHN WILKES BOOTH

Many people believe that President Lincoln's assassin, John Wilkes Booth, was not the man who was shot in a Virginia barn on April 14, 1865. Over the following decades, some forty men have "confessed" to being the infamous assassin.

Former Actor Gets Top Billing at Carnival Sideshows!

One such confessor, known as David E. George, committed suicide at Enid, Oklahoma, in 1903. Finis Bates, a shrewd lawyer from Memphis, Tennessee, obtained George's long-unclaimed but remarkably embalmed body. Identifying the body as John St. Helen, Bates claimed that the dead man had earlier confessed his true identity to him. Bates published this "true" story in *The Escape and Suicide of John Wilkes Booth*, and for years, the mummy of "Booth" was exhibited at carnival sideshows. The mummy superficially resembled the actor-turned-assassin, and it even had fractures and wounds similar to Booth's. Nevertheless, when the *Dearborn* [Michigan] *Independent* investigated the mummy in 1910, it was debunked as a fraud.

Amazing Disappearing Acts

AIMÉE SEMPLE McPHERSON'S KIDNAPPING

Aimée Semple McPherson (1890-1944) was a popular American evangelist in the 1920s and 1930s. In 1926, at the peak of her fame, she suddenly disappeared. According to newspaper reports, she had been swimming in the Pacific Ocean off Los Angeles, California, when she vanished; five weeks later, in the desert of Mexico, she suddenly reappeared.

Woman Evangelist Vanishes to Romantic Seaside Resort!

On May 18, 1926, McPherson invited her mother, Minnie Kennedy, to accompany her to the beach. When her mother declined, McPherson went instead with her secretary, Emma Schaffer. After seeing McPherson far out in the water, Schaffer eventually lost track of her boss. Later, when McPherson did not return to shore, Schaffer spread the word that she had drowned.

An extensive search, however, produced no body. The newspapers were teeming with questions and reported sightings of the evangelist in small California towns. The police, meanwhile, had received a number of ransom demands, but they, too, were viewed with skepticism. Nonetheless, Kennedy offered a $25,000 reward for the return of her daughter alive.

Five weeks after the disappearance, the Los Angeles police received a call that McPherson had surfaced in Douglas, Arizona. A little while later, the errant evangelist phoned home. Kennedy warned her daughter not to speak to anyone about her "kidnapping." By the time her mother arrived in Arizona, however, McPherson had been downright chatty with the paparazzi.

Aimée Semple McPherson.

Aimée claimed to have been abducted and tortured after having been lured to a car parked by the beach by someone who told her a story about a dying infant. Once inside the car, she was overcome by chloroform. When she awoke, she was bound to a cot—somewhere in northern Mexico.

Her escape could have taught James Bond a thing or two: She rolled off the cot, cut her bonds with a discarded tin can, and finally managed to climb out a window. She then walked through miles of desert to the Mexican border town of Agua Prieta, just across from Douglas, where she collapsed.

An unlikely story. Not surprisingly, not everyone lent a sympathetic ear. The press, in particular, questioned her story. After all, how—after dragging through miles of scorching desert heat—could Aimée emerge without sunburn or injury? And she wasn't even thirsty. What's more, her clothing wasn't torn, and there were grass stains on her shoes.

Word began to spread that Kenneth Ormiston, McPherson's radio station engineer, had been seen with her at a seaside resort during the time in question. Ormiston and the evangelist had been linked romantically before, and his wife had threatened to name McPherson as the reason she was seeking a divorce from her husband. Apparently, Kennedy ended the scandal by forcing Ormiston out of his job; after he had left the area, she then paid him to come back to Los Angeles during a time when it was rumored that he was traveling in Europe with McPherson.

McPherson claimed that her kidnappers had cut off some of her hair to send to her mother, along with a demand for a $500,000 ransom. Kennedy did receive an envelope containing a lock of hair, along with a demand for that amount of money; if the ransom was not paid, the note said, McPherson would be sold into white slavery in Mexico. The police questioned the note's authenticity.

Both Aimée McPherson and Minnie Kennedy were called before a Los Angeles grand jury formed to investigate the incident. The grand jury found enough evidence to try them for "conspiracy to perpetuate a hoax," and Kennedy was arrested for obstruction of justice. During the days leading up to the trial, much money changed hands in order to influence key players in the case. At the eleventh hour, the district attorney decided that no one would be well served by a trial, and he dropped all charges. The public, however, did not forget.

AMBROSE BIERCE AND RELATED DISAPPEARANCE TALES

Ambrose Bierce (1842-1913) was known in literary circles as a journalist, wit, cynic, and writer of creepy tales of horror and death. He is

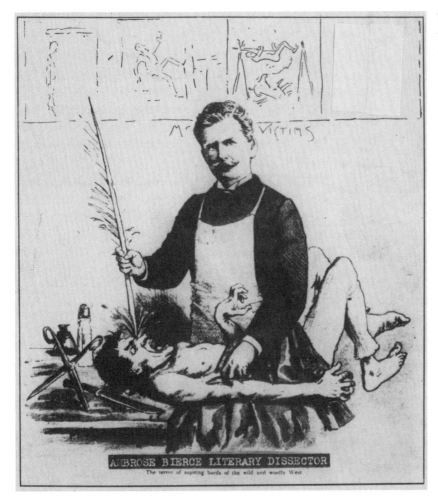

Wordsmith Bierce was lampooned in the early 1890s.

AMBROSE BIERCE LITERARY DISSECTOR
The terror of aspiring bards of the wild and woolly West

also known for having vanished in 1913, never to be found again. A veteran hoaxer, Bierce probably orchestrated his own mysterious disappearance—but investigators will never know for sure. What they do know is that Bierce's stories inspired more than a few bizarre—and suspicious—tales of inexplicable disappearances.

Writer Vanishes Without Trace!

Bierce was a very persuasive writer. In *Can Such Things Be?* he convinced many readers that his accounts were authentic, or at least based on true events. But research indicates otherwise; in fact, the author himself wrote, "With a hardy mendacity that I now blush to remember I gave names, dates and places with a minute particularity which seemed to authenticate the narratives that I came near to a belief in

HE BLINDED THEM WITH SCIENCE

In "Science to the Front," Bierce relates the crackpot theories of "Dr. Hern of Leipsic." Hern, a product of Bierce's imagination, had a theory: "In the visible world there are void places," he claimed, rather like "cells in Swiss cheese." These cheeselike void places, it seems, are somehow responsible for mysterious disappearances. Hern's cheese theory, not surprisingly, didn't cut it with the scientific poobahs.

some of them myself." On one occasion, Bierce cowrote a book, *The Dance of Death*, in which he pretended to condemn the waltz as "shameless." Then, using a phoney name, he wrote a column that discredited and panned the book.

The end of a pleasant correspondence. There is plenty of evidence to suggest that "the Old Trickster," as Bierce was known, planned his own disappearance. In fact, Bierce once wrote an essay supporting suicide as a way to avoid a decrepit old age; he also told his publisher that he owned a German revolver for just such a purpose. Bierce selected a location in the Colorado River gorge where his corpse would be protected from vultures. In farewell letters to his friends, he made dramatic statements such as, "This is to say good-by at the end of a pleasant correspondence" and

A FAINT VOICE CRYING FOR HELP

David Lang walked into his pasture on September 23, 1880, and—in full view of his wife, children, and a family friend—vanished. The shocked onlookers immediately ran to the spot where he was last seen, but no trace of the Tennessee farmer remained. No hole or any other clue offered an explanation for the mysterious disappearance. As time passed, a circle of stunted grass marked the spot where Lang was last seen; sometimes, from within the circle, family members heard his voice faintly calling for help.

Again, historical research fails to substantiate the story. In fact, there was no evidence of any farmer named Lang. There is, however, a first-person account by Sarah Emma Lang, who claimed to be David Lang's daughter. Her account, "How Lost Was My Father?," appeared in the July 1953 issue of *Fate* magazine. The story turned out to be a hoax. Nevertheless, Lang claimed to communicate with her father through "automatic writing" (a form of mediumship in which one enters an altered state of consciousness, allowing the hand to write without conscious direction).

The story of David Lang, like the stories of Oliver Larch, derived from Ambrose Bierce's trilogy; in this case, the source was "The Difficulty of Crossing a Field," which describes the witnessed vanishing of an Alabama planter named Williamson.

Heroes, Bad Guys, and Impostors

"My work is finished, and so am I." Bierce also wrote to his daughter to give up his cemetery plot: "I do not wish to lie there," he wrote, "That matter is all arranged and you will not be bothered about the mortal part of [signed] Your Daddy."

Bierce made it look as though he was traveling to Mexico, possibly to serve with Pancho Villa (Mexican bandit and revolutionary leader). After he disappeared, supposedly after leaving Chihuahua, Mexico, the American consul investigated; there was no evidence, however, that Bierce had ever been there. Privately, the Old Trickster confessed, "You need not believe all that these newspapers say of me and my purposes. I had to tell them something." He also vowed in a letter, "And nobody will find my bones"; no one ever has.

THE BERMUDA TRIANGLE

Vincent Gaddis coined the term "Bermuda Triangle" in 1964 to describe an area in the Atlantic Ocean roughly bound by Puerto Rico, the Bahamas, and the tip of Florida. Gaddis—a self-made "researcher" who promoted the "mystery" of spontaneous human combustion—suggested that the Bermuda Triangle spelled doom for all who ventured into its domain, and other writers since Gaddis have continued to sensationalize the story. Inspired by the disappearance of several dozen ships and planes in "the Devil's triangle," scads of writers have speculated about "time warps," UFO kidnappings, and other equally bizarre "theories."

> ### BERMUDA GEOMETRY
>
> Vincent Gaddis later regretted coining the term "Bermuda Triangle" since "a triangle implies boundaries that contain the phenomena." Others have called it an oval or even a trapezoid (a figure with four unequal sides). Author Richard Winer favors the latter term: "The first four letters of the word trapezium," he points out, "more than adequately describe it."

Devil's Triangle Decimates Teams of Tankers and Torpedo Bombers!

On the clear and sunny afternoon of December 5, 1945, Flight 19, a group of Avenger torpedo bombers, vanished. The five bombers left Fort Lauderdale Naval Air Station for a routine two-hour patrol; instead, after a few brief radio exchanges with other planes and ground receivers, all five planes disappeared. Headed for the last estimated position of Flight 19, a giant Martin Mariner plane with a crew of thirteen also vanished; no trace of any of the six planes has ever been found.

Nevertheless, in *The Bermuda Triangle Mystery—Solved*, reference librarian Lawrence David Kusche concluded that the so-called triangle was "a manufactured mystery." Citing a Navy investigation's report on the fate of Flight 19, Kusche showed that the patrol was made up of rook-

ies; what's more, their leader was obviously disoriented and had changed direction a number of times during the four hours the squadron was lost. And other factors—such as the approach of bad weather, poor radio reception, a failed teletype, and a military rule that required the planes to stay together—contributed to the squadron's desperate situation.

Kusche believes that the planes ran out of gas and were forced to ditch at sea during a stormy night. "Had any one of these factors not prevailed," he says, "the flight might have ended differently. One or more of the planes might have made it back, and the event would have been forgotten, rather than becoming known as the strangest flight in the history of aviation."

As for the Martin Mariner, its disappearance is no real mystery: Dubbed "flying gas tanks" because of the dangerous fumes that were often present in the fuselage, the planes sometimes burst into flames when a spark or a crew member's cigarette ignited the fumes. And, contrary to popular belief, the Mariner was not the only plane that searched

Flight 19—a group of Avenger torpedo bombers like these—vanished into thin air on December 5, 1945.

for the lost patrol: Other planes left *before* and *after* the Mariner, and returned unscathed.

Public Mystery Number One Debunked. Kusche has debunked a number of Bermuda Triangle "mysteries." For example, an abandoned ship was found drifting off the Florida coast in 1944; the puzzle fell in place when a hurricane—omitted from most writers' accounts—was restored to the scenario. A plane that allegedly vanished in the Triangle in 1950 actually exploded in 1951, some 600 miles west of Ireland. And yet another plane, a British troop transport that disappeared in 1953 "north of the Bermuda Triangle" probably crashed in torrential rain and wind some **900 miles north** of the Triangle.

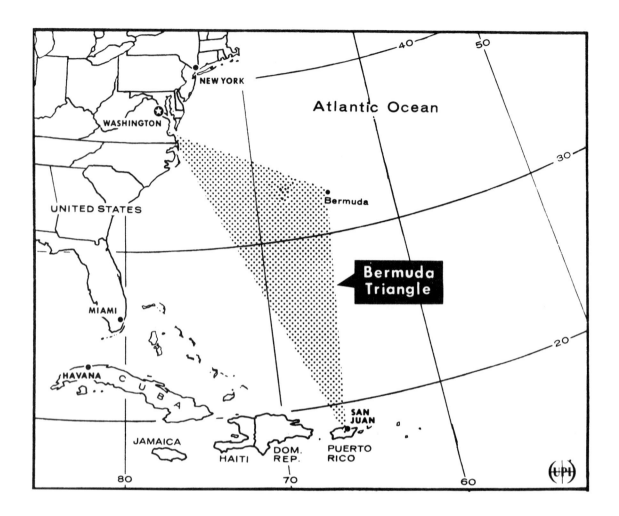

Some say the Bermuda Triangle is really more of a trapezoid.

Kusche summed up the situation thus: "Previous writers, either on purpose or because they were gullible, created the mystery. I found that many things writers call mysterious really aren't if you take the trouble to dig for some information. Previous writers on this topic had to be either very poor researchers with little curiosity, very gullible, or outright sensationalists. They've been passing off their own lack of information as mysteries."

The Sulphur Queen Vanishes

The S.S. *Marine Sulphur Queen* supposedly vanished in the Triangle in early February 1963. The tanker, en route from Beaumont, Texas, was last heard from at 1:25 A.M. on February 4, as it neared the Straits

A life preserver (tied to a man's shirt) and a life jacket—stenciled with the words S.S. *Sulphur Queen*—were surrounded by sharks when they were plucked from the Atlantic Ocean.

of Florida. On February 9, when it was one day overdue at Norfolk, Virginia, the *Sulphur Queen* became the focus of an air and sea search. Over the following days, the search was widened, but no corpses, lifeboats, or oil slicks provided any clue as to the tanker's mysterious misfortune.

Eventually, some wreckage did surface, proving that the vessel did not simply vanish: Patrollers found a piece of an oar and other debris from the tanker, including a name board that bore the letters "ARINE SULPH" between its shattered ends. The fact that the tanker did not send a distress message suggests that whatever happened happened suddenly. The vessel was structurally weak, plagued by fires, and probably encountered rough weather. With a cargo of 15,260 tons of molten sulphur, the ship might well have exploded—as did a similar vessel carrying liquid benzene in 1972—or it might simply have sunk in deep water.

Witchcraft on the Atlantic!

Still another touted Triangle mystery occurred in December 1967, when a twenty-three-foot cabin cruiser named *Witchcraft* disappeared with its two-man crew just off Miami Beach. The men reported a damaged propeller to the Coast Guard and asked to be towed back to port.

They also reported that the boat's hull was intact and that the built-in floatation chambers rendered the craft virtually unsinkable. Yet, when the Coast Guard reached the location—after only nineteen minutes had passed—there was no trace of the boat, the men, or their life preservers. It looked like the Triangle had claimed two more victims.

In truth—contrary to the way the incident is usually portrayed—the craft was disabled in rough weather amid six-foot waves. Without the use of its engine propeller to steer in the waves, the boat could easily have been swamped. What's more, since the Coast Guard did not know the exact position of the craft, patrollers were forced to conduct a nighttime search over an enormous area. In short, there is no reason to believe that the *Witchcraft* fell under the deadly spell of the Devil's Triangle.

Heroes, Bad Guys, and Impostors

You Can't
Believe
Everything
You Read

Literary Lies

BENJAMIN FRANKLIN'S HOAXES

Benjamin Franklin (1706-1790) had a mischievous sense of humor. Known for his wit and wisdom, Franklin was an inveterate hoaxer; most of his ruses were literary, and nearly all imparted some kind of moral lesson.

Founding Father Franklin Fabricated Fabulous Fables!

In 1730, Franklin published a hoax in his own paper, the *Pennsylvania Gazette*. The article, titled "A Witch Trial at Mount Holly"—supposedly a news story from New Jersey—claimed that about 300 people gathered at the town of Mount Holly in order to watch a test of a man and a woman accused of witchcraft. The charge: "Making their neighbors' sheep dance ... and ... causing hogs to speak and sing Psalms." The test involved placing the accused on one pan of a large balance scale, with a large Bible placed on the other pan. Supposedly, the Bible would outweigh a witch.

In the actual test, the "witches" each weighed much more than the Bible, but the spectators still insisted that the witch suspects be given the water test. Thrown into a pond, both suspects floated—indicating their guilt, since an innocent person was supposed to sink. The judges decided to test the suspects again—this time without their clothes—when the weather was warmer. At this point, Franklin's parody of a witchcraft trial ended.

A skilled printer, Ben Franklin created the Gospel according to Ben.

The Gospel according to Ben. In the beginning, Franklin created a book. And Franklin said let there be an extra chapter, and there was an extra chapter. And Franklin saw the extra chapter, that it was good ...

and Franklin called the extra chapter the fifty-first chapter of the First Book of Moses called Genesis.

Franklin's skills as a printer came in handy as a hoaxer. Writing with biblical flair, he added a fifty-first chapter to Genesis, creating his own version of the Old Testament. Franklin's chapter tells the story of how Abraham offered a stranger shelter; when the stranger told Abraham that he worshiped a different god, however, Abraham drove him from his house. After God appeared to Abraham to tell him that he had acted incorrectly, Abraham found the man and returned him to the hospitality of his home. People claimed that they had never seen this chapter of Genesis before; nevertheless, it *was* in Franklin's copy of the Old Testament, and it *did* sound authentic.

The slave trade and Christians in Algeria. Another of Franklin's hoaxes was a satirical attack on slavery. In a letter to the *Federal Gazette*—which had recently published an article reporting an emotional speech by a Georgia congressman urging Congress not to interfere with the slave trade—Franklin wrote that the Congressman's speech reminded him of another speech. That speech, he wrote, had been delivered 100 years earlier by one Sidi Mehemet Ibrahim of Algeria.

Ibrahim defended the enslavement of Christians in Algeria, claiming that it was not wrong to enslave them because they were slaves in their own countries, where despots ruled. Those who proposed that the Christians be set free were misguided, he said, because the Christians were too ignorant to govern themselves; if the slave Christians were freed, they would raise trouble and endanger the government. The parallels with the congressman's speech were obvious, but no Algerian named Ibrahim ever delivered any such speech. Franklin, it seems, had fabricated the speech to make a point.

Count Schaumbergh's letter to the Redcoats. To emphasize the evil of recruiting Hessian soldiers (German mercenary soldiers) to fight with the Brit-

---

POOR RICHARD SAYS THE COMPETITION IS DEAD

Using the name "Poor Richard Saunders," Ben Franklin published a satirical book titled *Poor Richard's Almanac*. Spoofing astrology, he predicted the death of a rival almanac editor named Titan Leeds, pinpointing the day and even the hour of his rival's demise. When the announced time passed, Leeds vigorously denied that he was dead. Poor Richard, however, was just as stubborn in insisting that he was dead: For eight years, he swore that Titan Leeds was no more. When Leeds finally did die, Poor Richard said that the friends of Titan had finally decided to admit that their comrade had, in fact, checked into the great library in the sky.

BENJAMIN FRANKLIN'S EPITAPH FOR HIMSELF

The body of
Benjamin Franklin, printer,
(Like the cover of an old book,
Its contents worn out,
And stript of its lettering and gilding)
Lies here, food for worms!
Yet the work itself shall not be lost,
For it will, as he believed,
    appear once more
In a new
And more beautiful edition,
Corrected and amended
By its Author!

ish against the Americans in the Revolutionary War, Franklin wrote a hoax letter. In it, he claimed to be "Count Schaumbergh"—much like Count Schaumburg who was in charge of recruiting the Hessians. "Schaumbergh" reported that he was angry because the figures stating how many Hessians were killed in battle were understated. Since he received money for each Hessian killed, he wanted to know the correct figures in order to avoid being cheated out of any money. The British replied that the undercount was due to a number of wounded who were not counted as dead. Schaumbergh then insisted that since these men could no longer fight, the surgeons should make no effort to save them. This didn't make the count look very good, and British sentiment began to turn against the continued recruitment of Hessian soldiers.

Polly Baker, model mom. The Polly Baker case was possibly Ben Franklin's most influential hoax. Baker—who had five children born out of wedlock—was five times convicted of immorality. Following her last conviction, Polly appealed to the court. Her speech—reprinted many times and recounted in articles that began appearing in 1760—asked for the equal treatment of women before the law.

Polly pointed out that she supported all of her children and never turned down a proposal of marriage (the one she accepted led to her first pregnancy, at which point her husband-to-be abandoned her). She also believed that the country needed to boost its population. Finally, Polly appealed to simple math: She would be better able to support her children, she said, if the court would stop fining her for every baby born out of wedlock. She also insisted that her actions hurt no one, and she noted that no action was taken against the men in each case—each of whom was as responsible as she.

Apparently, the story of Polly Baker struck a nerve: For years, it was republished in newspapers and magazines all over the world. But the story of Polly Baker wasn't exactly true: Franklin—who always had a moral in mind—penned the parable of Polly Baker. He seems to have modeled his story after the case of a real woman, Eleanor Kellog, who was convicted of immorality five times between 1733 and 1745, in Worcester, Massachusetts; the speech to the court, however, was strictly a Franklin fabrication.

THE SILENCE OF BEN FRANKLIN

Franklin's first known hoax was a series of letters published in the *New-England Courant*. In these fourteen letters—written in 1722 when Franklin was only sixteen years old—the young writer posed as a cheerful but shrewd rural widow named Silence Dogood. Dogood poked fun at drunkenness, pride, and hoop petticoats, and she favored life insurance to help support widowed women. Benjamin's brother James was the editor of the *Courant*—but there's no evidence that he knew that "Silence" was brother Ben's pen-name-in-drag.

EDGAR ALLAN POE'S HOAXES

Once upon a midnight dreary, while I pondered, weak and weary,

Over many a quaint and curious volume of forgotten lore,

While I nodded, nearly napping, suddenly there came a tapping,

As of some one gently rapping, rapping at my chamber door.

—*The Raven*, 1845

Edgar Allan Poe (1809–1849) was best known as an American poet and short story writer. Few people have not heard of Poe's *The Fall of the House of Usher, The Murders in the Rue Morgue, The Tell-Tale Heart*, and *The Raven*; but not everyone is aware of the fact that Poe was a serious hoaxer, responsible for at least a half-dozen scams—some of which unfolded long after he was dead and buried.

Man Flies to Moon to Escape Creditors!

In 1835, Poe published installments of "The Unparalleled Adventures of One Hans Pfaall" in the *Southern Literary Messenger*. As the story goes, a man built a balloon and flew to the moon in order to escape his creditors. After a number of adventures, he landed at his lunar destination, where he lived among the moon's inhabitants for five years. Eventually, a moon person was sent to earth with a message: Pfaall would like to return to the earth, but on two conditions. To begin with, the prodigal earthling demanded a large payment for his story; and he wanted to be forgiven for all his past crimes—including the murders of three of his creditors. Although the earth officials were willing to comply, the moon person began to fear the earthlings and left before he had their response.

Poe also planned to describe the moon and its inhabitants in great detail, but just as he was about to continue with the dubious adventures of Hans Pfaall, a British writer by the name of Richard

You Can't Believe Everything You Read

Edgar Allan Poe,
a well-versed hoaxer.

Adams Locke completed a celebrated series of hoax articles claiming that the moon shelters "a vast population of human beings." Beaten to the punch, Poe abandoned his lunar ruse.

"Leonainie" quoth the poet never. A poem named "Leonainie" has repeatedly been attributed to Edgar Allan Poe. Written in Poe-like handwriting and style—and signed "E.A.P."—it was supposedly found in a book in a hotel room; the writer, it seems, had left the poem in lieu of paying for his room and board.

Although the book in which it was found was real enough, the poem—as a number of Poe experts testified—was definitely not the work of author of *The Raven*. "Leonainie" was in fact a poor imitation of Poe's style penned by poet James Whitcomb Riley (1849-1916). A fair poet in his own right, Riley soon confessed that the poem was his, and even included "Leonainie" in *Armazindy*, an anthology of his poems. This did not, however, discourage others from continuing to insist that the poem was a genuine Poe piece.

Alfred R. Wallace was a stubborn man: He refused, in spite of overwhelming evidence, to admit that Poe did not write "Leonainie." Long after the poem had been correctly attributed to Riley, Wallace received a handwritten copy from his brother in California, who supposedly claimed that the poem was Poe's. Wallace, it seems, was unaware that the correct authorship of the poem had been revealed twenty years earlier; he even went so far as to claim that Riley had passed Poe's work off as his own.

SHAKESPEARE HOAXES

Many people agree that William Shakespeare (1564–1616) penned some of the best known stories ever written. The author of poems, love stories, comedies, and tragedies, he's been called the greatest writer in the English language; yet not much is known about the man called the Bard. What is known about him does not suggest that he was brilliant or educated. Because of this, many scholars have attempted to "prove" that someone other than William Shakespeare wrote the Bard's plays.

Shakespeare "Play" Makes Bard Roll Over in His Grave!

Samuel Ireland, a retired silk weaver, was comfortably situated. He had enough money to indulge in his hobbies of rare book and curio collecting. His special interest, however, was William Shakespeare. Ireland zealously collected Shakespearean relics, and his son, William Henry (1777-1835), was eager to help. There was a problem, however; real Shakespearean items did not exist, so William Henry created his own historic relics.

William Henry Ireland forged a number of items, including a deed with Shakespeare's name on it, a Confession of Faith by Shakespeare, and a love letter to Anne Hathaway. Although the elder Ireland was con-

William Shakespeare.

vinced of the authenticity of these items, they now appear to be clumsy forgeries.

William Henry Ireland's biggest hoax involved producing a previously unknown Shakespearean play, *Vortigern and Rowena*. After the play was "discovered," Ireland succeeded in getting Richard Brinsley Sheridan to produce it, and John Philip Kemble, a great Shakespearean actor, agreed to star in the play. *Vortigern and Rowena* was scheduled to open on April Fool's Day, 1796, but the production was delayed until

The audience thought that *Vortigern* was so bad that they applauded the announcement that it would not be performed again. According to one account, some of the actors' lines—notably "Oh that this solemn mockery should end"— were repeated back by the audience.

the next day. Two days before *Vortigern and Rowena* was staged, Edmund Malone, a prominent Shakespearean scholar of the time, published a book in which he denounced the play as a forgery and a hoax. Nonetheless, the performance sold out; it was so bad, however, that the play was not performed again.

Ireland never sold any of his forgeries. Since he produced them for the benefit of his father, he was never forced to answer any criminal charges. Although both father and son were at one time suspected of the forgeries, young Ireland fessed up; in 1796, he wrote a short confession as a pamphlet, followed in 1806 by a longer, book-length confession.

Forgery in the Ivory Tower. John Payne Collier (1789-1883) was a highly respected scholar, but in 1852, when an annotated copy of Shakespeare's Second Folio was examined, he was soon suspected of fraud. Collier had "discovered" the Shakespearean book—known as the Perkins Folio from the ownership inscription—in which thousands of corrections had supposedly been made in a handwriting that appeared to be contemporary with Shakespeare's. Since the First Folio printing of Shakespeare's collected works contained so many printing errors, the idea of a "corrected text"—supposedly from an authoritative hand—intrigued Shakespeare scholars.

Why did the Perkins Folio excite so much interest? The "corrector" of the text was, after all—at best—a sixteenth-century John Doe. It seems Collier himself inspired the public's interest in the inferior folio: He touted his discovery as a pivotal find, and incorporated the corrections into a new edition of Shakespeare (which sold very well).

At first, Collier never allowed the Perkins Folio to be examined out of his sight, and eventually, he refused to allow it to be examined at *all*. In 1858, however, Collier was forced to give in, and the staff of the British Museum examined the book. Their verdict: The Perkins Folio was a forgery and a hoax. Collier's reputation plunged, and his earlier work on the Bard was carefully scrutinized. Documents relating to Shakespeare that Collier had claimed to have discovered in the Bridgewater Library some twenty years earlier were found to be forgeries. Additionally, the manuscripts on which Collier had based his three most famous books on Shakespeare, too, were pronounced to be bogus Bard deeds. Collier, who had access to all of the famous collections of Shakespeare materials, was accused of planting forgeries among them; he protested his innocence, but spent the last thirty years of his life in disgrace.

Dewey Ganzel reexamined the evidence in the case, and concluded that Collier was really an innocent victim. As it turns out, Collier's chief accuser was Clement Ingleby, a man who was involved in a conspiracy against the scholar. Ingleby—Ganzel says—actually knew that Collier was innocent; he was convinced that the only way to do away with the Perkins' "corrections" to the Shakespeare text would be to discredit Collier completely. Ingleby, it seems, felt that the corrections were unforgivable corruptions of the Bard's perfect pearls of wisdom. Although Ganzel does make a good case for believing that Ingleby was something less than an honest man, the final verdict on John Payne Collier is still out. It's possible that Collier was, indeed, a Shakespearean hoaxer; but it's equally possible that Ingleby, or the forger of the Shakespeare text—possibly Sir Frederic Madden—were the hoaxers. In fact, it's possible that they were all involved in the scam.

Seeing
Isn't Always
Believing

Painting by Numbers

IS THERE SUCH A THING AS A PERFECT CRIME?

Once a forgery is accepted as genuine, it can't help but affect the historical understanding of art from that time. Is it possible to create a perfect, undetectable forgery? We'll never know; if there are any truly successful forgeries out there, they're hanging, to this day, on museum walls.

LADY FORGERS

Some women have been forgers, such as Madame Claude Latour, who was convicted by a French court in 1947. Some of her Utrillo forgeries were said to be so accurate that even Utrillo himself couldn't be sure he hadn't painted them.

FORGERIES

Forgery is normally defined as a work of art that is presented to a buyer or audience with the intention to deceive. This fraudulent intention distinguishes forgeries from honest copies and mistaken attributions. Usually a forger paints a work in the style of a famous artist and tries to sell it, often in conjunction with an unscrupulous art dealer, claiming that it is by the hand of a famous artist. Forgers seldom try to execute exact copies of existing authentic paintings since such works are practically impossible to sell to informed buyers.

Everything You Always Wanted to Know About Forgery But Were Afraid to Ask!

It is possible to discern a vague pattern by studying the more noted forgers of the last century. Forgers—most of whom are men—tend to be artists whose once-promising careers have faltered. Successful forgers often possess impressive technical skills, but, as artists, seem to have no original ideas. They use talent to imitate another artist's style; while the painting may resemble the intended work, it often lacks the inner passion and vision that animates great art.

The imitative ability of the forger succeeds best where a single fake is seen in isolation. A whole gallery or portfolio of forgeries, on the other hand, is more apt to betray itself as forgery. Many forgers attempt to fake sketches and "early works" of an artist because such works can be said to have been completed before the artist established his or her mature, confident—and most recognizable—style.

There's more to forgery than meets the eye. Creating a plausible forgery is a complicated process. If a forger wishes, for example, to fake an important seventeenth-century painting, he must begin with a seventeenth-century canvas; it would be virtually impossible to create an old-looking canvas from modern materials. After finding an old—but unimportant—painting, the forger must either paint over the original or dissolve and scrape away the old painting.

A forgery that is painted over an old painting can be discovered if the underpainting is detected in an X-ray analysis. Trying to remove the old paint from the canvas, on the other hand, may be next to impossible, since chemicals can fuse with the fibrous material. Sometimes, forgers leave parts of the underpainting that cannot be removed, incorporating them into the design of the new forgery.

In selecting paints and brushes, the forger of a seventeenth-century painting must know the history of pigment formulas and must carefully avoid using paints that were invented after the supposed date of composition in order to avoid revealing the fraud. For example, the color ultramarine did not come into general use until 1838, and Prussian blue does not pre-date 1800.

Style is all. Style is of great importance. A forger must study the brush techniques, typical subject matter, and stylistic qualities of the artist to be forged. Many forgeries are pastiche works—paintings that draw together miscellaneous elements from a number of authentic paintings in a way that fits perfectly into the established style of the older artist.

Style is, however, where even the most technically accomplished forgers usually fail. It is almost impossible for a modern painter to be able to duplicate the artistic conventions of an earlier century. Perhaps more importantly, it is next to impossible to avoid the influ-

A SMART INVESTMENT

Although many old paintings of little value have been "recycled" by forgers, mistakes have been known to happen. One story involves a dealer who tried to sell an "eighteenth-century French" painting to Alfred duPont, a wealthy industrialist, claiming that it was a portrait of one of duPont's ancestors. The asking price: $25,000—a major investment in 1931. When duPont grew suspicious, the painting dropped to $10,000, eventually falling to a mere $1,000. Since duPont considered the frame alone to be worth $400, he bought the portrait and showed it to a curator who determined that the work had been altered by overpainting. The curator suggested that the overpainting be removed; that done, the original painting turned out to be a magnificent *Madonna and Child* by the seventeenth-century Spanish painter Murillo—valued then at a whopping $150,000.

TWENTIETH-CENTURY PHOTOFORGERS

It would be very difficult for a twentieth-century artist to paint a picture without in some way being influenced by the invention of photography. But seventeenth-century painters knew nothing of photography, and their detailed paintings show it.

ence of conventions and discoveries that have occurred after the work was supposed to have been painted.

A pigment of the imagination. The pigment of old paintings, acquired through time, has two characteristics: It becomes quite hard and shrinks slightly, causing a network of fine cracks (blackened with dust and dirt) called craquelure. Depending on how thick the pigment is, it may take ten years or more for a forgery in oils to dry to the hardness of an old work. Impatient to cash in on their work, forgers sometimes add solvents to their paints to increase the drying speed.

Craquelure presents a more serious problem. Craquelure can be mimicked by painting fine, black cracks over the surface. This technique will not, however, get past the experienced eye of a dealer or curator. The forger may try to induce cracking in the paint surface by slow baking; but even if the baked-and-cooled painting is rolled on a tube, the cracks will tend to line up in one direction, rather than extend randomly in all directions.

The forger may also attempt to achieve the effect of a cracked surface by scratching into the pigment with a needle. When the resulting surface is wiped with black ink, the result can look excellent, but the "cracks" will not extend all the way into the canvas, which may reveal the fraud. It is possible to achieve a more natural cracking by mixing egg white with pigment; this is difficult, however, because it dries faster and requires the forger to work quickly.

Once a satisfactory appearance of craquelure has been achieved, the made-to-order masterpiece requires a final varnishing. Many collectors of old art consider it a mark of authenticity when a painting is clouded by a dark varnish. Finally, a light dusting of attic dust makes the painting appear more authentic.

Every picture needs a story. When the painting is finished, the forger faces what is perhaps the most difficult task. A seventeenth-century masterpiece doesn't suddenly appear out of nowhere: There must be a believable story to explain where the painting came from and why it remained undiscovered for so long. Where was the picture hiding for the last couple of centuries? Why didn't anyone know where it was? And why is it suddenly enjoying the limelight? These aren't questions that are easily answered. First, the forger needs to invent an origin for the object. This may involve creating one or two official museum certificates with old wax seals to be affixed to the back of the canvas; a deft forger who has the skill to fake a seventeenth-century painting would have little trouble faking old certificates of authenticity.

If the forgery is of a twentieth-century work, it is sometimes possible to trick the painter's relatives—or even to exercise a little financial persuasion—to get them to sign a letter of authenticity. The forger—or the forger's dealers and partners—then needs to come up with a story of how a long-lost painting happened to fall into his/her hands. Most stories are a variation on the following theme: "The old Italian family who owned this picture for generation after generation has fallen upon dire times and must sell the prized painting for financial reasons. The family insists on the utmost discretion—for the sake of their reputation—and must not, under any circumstances, be identified." Surely, anyone who would question such a tale of woe could not really be interested in purchasing the painting.

How much is that Picasso in the window? The price at which a forgery is offered to potential buyers is often an indication of its true status. Authentic masterpieces are never a bargain, but honest copies are cheap. Forgeries offered by fraudulent dealers tend to be priced far too high for copies, but considerably below the market value of an authentic work. How does the dealer account for this deep discount rate for a bona-fide masterpiece? The painting's owner, no doubt, has humongous debts and desperately needs immediate payment—even if it means taking a loss, as it were, on the true value of the painting.

The golden age of forgery. The nineteenth century was the heyday of forgery, when interest in classical antiquities and the Middle Ages was at an all-time high. The market for Old Masters paintings flour-

THE LOAVES, THE FISHES, AND THE COROT TABLEAUX

Landscape artist Jean-Baptiste-Camille Corot (1796-1875) was perhaps the most forged painter in history. It's been said—in jest—that of the 3,000 or so paintings he produced in his career, about 10,000 are now in the United States. In fact, according to estimates, a group of Corot fakes are floating around the art world—to the tune of 100,000 inferior masterpieces. Many of his paintings feature a loose, sketchy, spontaneous style that lends itself to casual forgery. Besides being an extremely popular and prolific artist of his time, Corot was generous to the point of occasionally signing his own signature to his students' paintings. The body of work attributed to Corot is now so cluttered with fakes—some obvious and others subtle and respectable—that experts may never be able to sort out the Master from the forger.

ished, while imperial expansion created a fascination with art and craft objects from cultures beyond the "accepted" edge of civilization. Wealthy art collectors, not always quick to spot a fake, greedy dealers, and highly skilled craftsmen helped forgery to thrive as it never had. Objects that supposedly came from ancient Egypt, India, and the Far East were especially popular, as were works from medieval Europe.

The broad range of areas of interest inspired forgers to create new genres—or styles—of art. For example, Europe was providing ivory in considerable quantities; this, combined with the popularity of medieval carvings, resulted in the creation of scores of religious carvings in ivory that supposedly dated back to the Middle Ages. Meanwhile, authentic medieval ivories lost much of their popularity among collectors because of their confusion with twentieth-century fakes.

Large numbers of forgeries of African art are currently surfacing. Workshops within Africa are producing forgeries of nineteenth-century masks, ancestral figures, and artifacts capable of fooling even the most knowledgeable experts. Since the styles of African art are many, artificial aging techniques are straightforward, and prices are high, the current market is rife with "old" African pieces of dubious authenticity.

TWENTIETH-CENTURY ART FORGER

Hans van Meegeren (1889-1947), the most notorious and celebrated forger of the twentieth century, was born in the Dutch town of Deventer. Fascinated by drawing as a child, he pursued art in spite of his father's disapproval, sometimes spending all of his pocket money on art supplies. Once in high school, he finally received professional instruction and later went on to study architecture.

Van Meegeren Earns Millions Painting Fakes!

In 1911, van Meegeren married Anna de Voogt, and the couple moved to The Hague, where the young painter received his art degree in 1914. For the next ten years, van Meegeren supported himself by giving drawing lessons and selling his own work, holding fairly well-received exhibitions in 1916 and 1922.

Van Meegeren's artistic style was essentially conservative: He painted Dutch scenes, religious paintings, the dimly lit interiors of old churches, sentimental portraits, and works full of mystical symbolism. One drawing, *Queen Juliana's Deer*, enjoyed great popularity on calendars and postcards. His political outlook was extremely conservative and bigoted, and he was opposed to all modernist tendencies in art. Although van Meegeren was successful as an artist, he began to distrust art critics, who were increasingly negative and condescending about his work.

The artist's first forgeries. In 1923, van Meegeren divorced Anna and became involved with Johanna Oerlemans, the estranged wife of art critic Karl de Boer. That same year, van Meegeren produced his first forgery, *Laughing Cavalier*, presented as the work of Frans Hals. Authenticated by an expert, the work fetched a good price at auction, but was soon detected as a forgery. Van Meegeren's involvement, however, went undetected.

Van Meegeren learned some valuable lessons from this episode, which contributed to the success of his first Vermeer forgery, *Lady and Gentleman at the Spinet*. Jan Vermeer was a seventeenth century Dutch painter. Produced in 1932, the painting was praised as a fine Vermeer by Professor Abraham Bredius, an eminent art historian. Also that year, van Meegeren left Holland and moved with his second wife Johanna to southern France.

For the next four years, van Meegeren supported himself by painting portraits. Meanwhile, he studied the formulas for seventeenth-century paints and experimented with ways to produce a pigment surface that had the hardness of old paint and displayed craquelure. Using volatile flower oils, he managed to perfect the technique, employing it in his greatest Vermeer forgery, *Christ and the Disciples at Emmaeus*, painted from 1936 to 1937.

WIFELY INFLUENCE

Shortly after van Meegeren married Anna de Voogt, his artistic talents were recognized: The young artist won first prize and a gold medal from the General Sciences Section of the Delft Institute of Technology for a drawing of a church interior. Although van Meegeren agreed to sell this drawing, his wife caught him making a copy of it to sell as the original. This was the first evidence of the artist's interest in forgery, even if he was forging his own work. Although Anna van Meegeren managed to persuade her husband to abandon this petty forgery, he soon went on to paint more ambitious fakes.

A DISTORTED VIEW OF HISTORY

Following the success of *Christ and the Disciples at Emmaeus*, van Meegren included more of himself and less of Vermeer in his subsequent forgeries. With each new forged masterpiece, he gained more acceptance among critics; eventually his style became intertwined with Vermeer's style. Van Meegren's last forgeries were hardly anything like authentic Vermeers, but since curators and buyers had been influenced by earlier forgeries, van Meegren's scam went undetected. Had his forgeries remained undiscovered, today's view of Vermeer's art would be wildly distorted.

A wonderful moment in the life of an art lover. Van Meegeren invented a story about an impoverished Italian family that had owned the painting for generations and did not want the family name revealed. He then set out to sell it through Dutch dealer B.A. Boon. When asked to authenticate the painting, Bredius beamed, in a 1937 issue of *Burlington Magazine*, that the discovery of Emmaeus was a "wonderful moment in the life of an art lover." He wrote:

> We have here a—I am inclined to say—the masterpiece of Johannes Vermeer of Delft ... quite different from his other paintings and yet every inch a Vermeer.... In no other picture by the great Master of Delft do we find such sentiment, such a profound understanding of the Bible story—a sentiment so nobly human, expressed through the medium of the highest art.

Not everyone, however, was as enthusiastic as Professor Bredius in proclaiming the painting to be the original work of the Dutch master. In fact, having seen the painting when it was unveiled in 1937, an agent of the New York dealer Duveen Brothers wired the following cable to his bosses across the Atlantic: "Seen today at Bank large Vermeer ... Christ's Supper at Emmaeus supposed belong private family certified by Bredius who writing article ... price pounds ninety thousand ... picture rotten fake." Fake or no fake, the painting was sold, with Bredius's authentication, to the Boymans Museum in Rotterdam, The Netherlands, for a hefty sum—equivalent today to about two million U.S. dollars. For his part, Van Meegeren received about two-thirds of the loot.

A portrait of the artist as a jailbird. At this point, van Meegeren, who now had more money than ever before, began to abuse alcohol and drugs, eventually becoming addicted to morphine. Although he had originally planned to confess his forgery to humiliate the critics who had praised the painting—and perhaps to demonstrate his contempt for critics in general—he instead forged two more Vermeer paintings.

Van Meegeren was arrested only days after the end of World War II on the serious criminal charge of having sold a Dutch National Treasure to the enemy. One of his fake Vermeers, *The Adulteress*, had ended up in the personal art collection of the Nazi Reichsmarshall Hermann Goering. Rather than face a long sentence for collaborating with the Nazis, he confessed to forgery—still a crime but no national offense.

At first, van Meegeren's claim to have forged *Emmaeus* and *The Adulteress* as well as four other "authentic" Vermeers was greeted with more than a little disbelief. But soon there was no denying the forgery. Van Meegeren himself proposed that he paint a "new" Vermeer while he sat in jail awaiting his trial; the resulting painting, *The Young Christ Teaching in the Temple* was clearly by the same hand as the other fakes.

Hans van Meegeren (seated alone in the box at left) listens to testimony at his trial for allegedly having bilked art lovers out of more than $2 million.

Van Meegeren's trial received international coverage. The artist portrayed himself as a man who simply loved to paint and whose career had been ruined by malicious critics. Having humiliated art critics—not to mention having scammed the Nazi leader who shelled out a tidy sum for the bogus opus—he became a folk hero, and the court treated him leniently. On November 12, 1947, he received the minimum sentence, one year's imprisonment. Just over one month later, however, on December 29, van Meegeren died from cardiac arrest.

DOG OR UNDERDOG?

Once van Meegeren was cheered as an underdog of the art world, his forgeries began to fetch whopping sums.

TWO HOAXERS: SMITH AND DE HORY

Paul Jordan Smith was the author of a number of books of fiction. He apparently disliked Picasso and a number of other artistic innovators, and, in 1924, tried to found a new school of art, the "Disumbrationist School." The next year, masquerading as a Russian named Pavel Jerdanovitch, he entered a painting of his in a French exhibition. Daubed in the "disumbrationist" style, the painting was called *Exaltation*. Soon, a French art journal wrote to ask for photographs of Jerdanovitch's other work. Caught in the thick of his fakery, Smith replied that he was too poor to afford photographs of his other work. Nevertheless, he did manage to provide a bogus biography of himself.

Art World Falls for Fraud and Fakery!

By now, several French art journals were praising "Jerdanovitch's" so-called disumbrationist paintings: His work looked, according to one critic, like "Gauguin, pop art, and Negro minstrelsy" combined. After three years, however, tired of his double life cum Russian artiste, Smith confessed his tale of trickery to a feature writer for the *Los Angeles Times*. On August 14, 1927, the *Times* told all about Pavel Jerdanovitch and phoney disumbrationism.

The Greatest Forger of Our Time!

Elmyr de Hory was born in Hungary in 1906. His early life is a mystery, complicated by his many pseudonyms, including Von Houry, Louis Cassou, L. E. Raynal, Hoffman, Herzog, and Dory-Bouton. He probably inherited some significant amount of money because no one ever saw him work at anything but art.

In 1946, de Hory sold one of his paintings to a woman who was convinced she was purchasing a Picasso; later, she sold the painting to a dealer as a Picasso. This gave de Hory a profitable idea: Why not forge the works of other artists? After moving to the United States, de Hory, a consummate copycat, used direct mail to sell forged Degas, Modigliani, Matisse, Renoir, and Braque paintings. In 1968, however, his scam hit a snag when a customer noticed that some of the paint was still wet on one of his paintings—a painting that should have been long dry.

De Hory later moved to the Mediterranean island of Ibiza in the Balearics. There, author Clifford Irving met him and decided to write a book about de Hory's life. It's not known whether de Hory supplied the information to Irving or whether the information came from elsewhere; it is known, however, that Irving's book is not entirely reliable. Nonetheless, the book—titled *Fake! The Story of Elmyr de Hory, The Greatest Art Forger of Our Time*—does tell of the intricate network of art dealers and middlemen who later sold de Hory's forgeries to trusting and gullible lovers of art. Someone, Irving claims, made a lot of money from de Hory's forgeries, but it probably wasn't de Hory.

There's No Business Like Business Like Show Business

Behind the Scenes

BACKWARD MASKING

IS PAUL DEAD?

The term backward masking is actually a misnomer applied to subliminal messages played backwards. "Backmasking" originally meant that loud music or lyrics were covering indistinct words in the background.

Some Fundamentalist Christian ministries—notably Gary Greenwald in the beginning—have suggested that Satan prodded rock groups to record satanic messages backwards (backward masking) over the soundtracks of a number of rock albums. The messages could supposedly be heard clearly when the record or tape was played backwards, sending subliminal (unconscious) messages to the brain when played forward.

Satan Speaks Through Rock 'n' Roll!

The concept of backward masking presents some questions. Assume, for the sake of argument, that some music somewhere does contain such messages. Is there any proof that people can understand, consciously or unconsciously, spoken messages that are played backwards? Obviously, if people can't understand, or even perceive, such messages, it doesn't matter much whether the messages exist or not.

In 1985, researchers Don Vokey and John Read conducted a well-controlled study in which they found that almost no one could consciously or unconsciously perceive or understand a backwards message, even one consisting of words that they already knew by heart. In other words, if a satanic backwards message were on a record, no one playing that record's message backwards would be able to understand it.

One might also ask whether ambiguous sounds can be interpreted as meaningful words, even when they are not intended. In 1984, researchers Throne and Himelstein demonstrated that a subject's interpretation of ambiguous stimuli is affected by what he or she expects to hear. In other words, someone warned about a satanic message on a record is more likely to find such a message than someone who has not been told to expect to hear a message.

A number of specific recordings have been accused of having satanic messages. Among the groups accused by Fundamentalists are the Beatles, Black Oak Arkansas, Electric Light Orchestra (ELO), Queen, Jefferson Starship, Led Zeppelin, Styx, the Eagles, the Rolling Stones, Venom, and Mötley Crüe. The backwards words supposedly include "It's better to reign in hell than to serve in heaven," "I love you said the Devil," and "Satan, move in our voices." It's possible that these so-called backwards words contain a message, but it's also possible that they're simply meaningless noises.

Some rock groups have intentionally recorded backwards lyrics as a sort of joke. For example, the group ELO has a backwards message on one of their albums that says, "The music is reversible, but time is not. Turn back, turn back, turn back." A Pink Floyd album track has this deliberate backwards message: "Congratulations! You've discovered the secret message. Please send your answer to Old Pink care of the funny farm."

The diabolical force of Christian rock. Many Fundamentalists claim that subliminal messages are present in Christian rock songs as well. Others say that since all rock music is inspired by the devil, any subliminal messages—even the pro-Christian ones supposedly found in some songs—are demonically produced. As a matter of fact, Jimmy Swaggart, a television evangelist, condemned "So-called Christian rock" as a "diabolical force undermining Christianity from within."

BEATLES HOAXES

In 1964, in the early days of Beatlemania, four young men from Liverpool, *Illinois*, grew their hair to the then current Beatle-length in preparation for the upcoming first series of American concerts by the Beatles. They learned to lip-synch Beatles songs, practiced British accents from movies, and convinced a friend to portray Brian Epstein, the Beatles manager; the phoney Epstein also played Beatles music backstage.

MORAL MUZAK

In 1978, Hal Becker invented a device that inserted audio subliminal messages into music tapes. His messages—played forward—were used by department stores at a very low volume in their background music. Studies indicated that, thanks to messages such as "I am honest," and "I will not steal," shoplifting decreased in the stores where the moral sound-bytes aired; it is unclear, however, how controlled these studies were.

BAREFOOT IN HEAVEN

At one point in the heyday of "Beatlemania," rumors of Paul McCartney's death were widespread. Part of the evidence: The *Abbey Road* album cover, where Paul alone is barefooted. The culprit: Possibly Russ Gibbs, a Detroit disk jockey, who aired the rumor on October 19, 1969.

DID ELVIS KNOW HE WOULDN'T BE ON TOUR?

Presley was scheduled to go on an extended tour the week after he died, but he didn't prepare in his usual manner.

- Although Presley did go to the dentist to have his teeth cleaned the night before he died, he did not have his graying hair and sideburns dyed, as he usually did before going on tour.

- Presley had gained so much weight that his concert costumes no longer fit, yet he didn't get measured for any new costumes for the upcoming tour.

Fake Fab Four Evades Federal Marshals!

The group started its tour in rural Illinois, but was soon playing Iowa, Montana, and other scenic spots before moving on to Boise, Idaho; and Moose Jaw, Saskatchewan, Canada. On May 24, 1964, the very night when the *faux* Beatles were to play a gig at Rapid City, South Dakota, the *real* Beatles made their third live appearance on the Ed Sullivan show. Waiting at the stage door of the auditorium, Federal marshals corralled the Illinois Fab Four, who were eventually forced to return their ill-gotten earnings in lieu of having to sing the jailhouse rock.

ELVIS

Born in 1935, Elvis Aron Presley was probably his generation's most popular singer up until the time he died at the age of forty-two. Rocked by the news of the death of "the King," many Presley fans refused to believe that the legendary pop star had met an untimely end. Scores of Presley sightings, supposed photographs, and even phone calls from the dead rock star have been reported since his death in 1977.

Elvis Lives!

The circumstances of his death only helped to fuel the mystery. On August 16, 1977, Presley was found unconscious on his bathroom floor in his house—Graceland—in Memphis, Tennessee. The ambulance attendants who removed the body did not recognize Presley. Some reports say he was dead when he was found, others say he was near death. All the photographs of the death scene have disappeared from the coroner's files. Some reports say Presley was nude; others say he wore pajamas, but not everyone agrees on what color they were.

Heart trouble—or coronary artery disease—was listed as the official cause of the death of Elvis Aron Presley. (Some claim, without much justification, that an autopsy was never performed.) At least sixty pounds overweight in August of 1977, Presley, who was rumored to be addicted to many prescription medications, may have died of an overdose. Ac-

There's No Business Like Show Business

ELVIS'S AUTOPSY—ANOTHER MYSTERY

Tennessee law requires an autopsy in all cases of death where no physician or witness is present. The results of an autopsy can be kept secret for fifty years.

- The coroner's office declared the case closed on the day that Presley died, before the results of the autopsy were known.
- The death certificate was issued several months after Presley's death, supposedly to replace a lost original.
- The official homicide report says the body was found unconscious. The medical examiner's report says rigor mortis had already set in when the body was found—which would mean the body had been dead for several hours.
- The contents of Presley's stomach were taken for analysis, but no analysis seems to have been done.
- The death certificate lists Presley's weight as 170 pounds (while some versions of the death certificate leave the weight blank). Two hundred fifty pounds would have been closer to the mark.
- A handwriting "expert" states that it is his opinion, after examining samples of Presley's handwriting, that the Medical Examiner's Report was filled out by none other than Presley himself. The medical examiner who was in charge at the time begs to differ.

cording to reports, the aging star took medication for high blood pressure, lupus (a disease that creates skin lesions), and glaucoma (a disease of the eye) in addition to amphetamines and tranquilizers.

Dead men don't sweat. Presley's death raised many doubts, all of which pointed to a single question: Did Presley fake his death? The singer's funeral didn't lay the question to rest: People commented that the body in the open casket didn't look exactly like Presley. A relative noticed that one of the King's sideburns seemed to be coming off. And the corpse appeared to be "sweating"; even under the sweltering Tennessee sun, dead men don't sweat.

Adding to the puzzle is an unconfirmed report that Presley's father, Vernon, acknowledged that the corpse didn't look like his son; he indicated that Presley was "Upstairs," explaining, "We had to show the fans something." What exactly was upstairs—a living fraud or a dead rock star—he didn't say.

Reports of Elvis's Death: Were They Greatly Exaggerated? Presley is reported to have read and been impressed by the book *The*

Elvis, performing at his last concert in March 1977.

Passover Plot by Hugh Schoenfield. The author speculates that Jesus faked his death by taking a drug that temporarily made him appear to be dead. No stranger to medications, Presley is supposed to have been an expert on prescription drugs. Oddly, no prescription medicines were found in his home; while Presley usually kept his prescriptions in a trailer outside the house, it is believed that his girlfriend cleaned up *before* calling the paramedics.

Why would Presley fake his death? One story claims that Presley—supposedly appointed as an agent of the Drug Enforcement Agency (DEA)—felt his life was threatened by individuals involved in organized crime. Presley was issued a DEA badge: he collected law enforcement badges. No one yet has been able to determine whether his life was in danger because of his DEA activities.

Unfinished business. Presley's life insurance money has never been collected. He was reportedly insured by Lloyd's of London—an exclusive British insurance agency that has issued policies to many entertainers—but the amount of insurance is unclear. Contributing to the loose ends surrounding Presley's

legacy, an inventory of the estate left by Presley fails to list many of his personal items, such as jewelry, diaries, personal photographs of his family, and pieces of furniture.

It is possible to make a case that Presley faked his death. But there is a lot of evidence stacked against the possibility that he is alive and well and living in the nineties. The autopsy report, the fact that Presley has not performed in public, the reports of relatives who saw the body— and the difficulty of pulling off a hoax involving death—leave the burden of proof with those who say that Presley is still alive. The disappearance of key documents might indicate a conspiracy or coverup; then again, it may be the work of souvenir hunters. Did someone pay off all of the police and coroner's office employees to silence them? Speculate is about all fans can do, unless, of course, the King calls a press conference.

MILLI VANILLI

In November 1990, the pop music world was startled with the announcement that the album *Girl You Know It's True*—the Grammy Award-winning singing group Milli Vanilli's first album, which sold over seven million copies—did not contain the group's voices. Frank Farian, the German producer of the album, decided to make the hoax public when the group told him that they wanted to sing on their next album.

Farian didn't like the idea of allowing the duo to sing; he summed up his sentiments, saying "that's not really what I want to use on my records." Farian had recorded the hit song "Girl You Know It's True," which gave the album its title, before he ever met Rob Pilatus and Fab Morvan, the lead singers from Milli Vanilli. In short, it was Farian's brainchild to create the dreadlocked duo by having Pilatus and Morvan lip-synch to the lyrics of anonymous artists.

Milli Vanilli Sez "Girl You Know It Isn't True"!

Brad Howell, Johnny Davis, and Charles Shaw aren't exactly household names. But the music they made was Top 40 fare. The National Academy of Recording Arts and Sciences awarded a Grammy to their song "Girl You Know Its True"—that is, until Milli Vanilli went down in the Hall of Shame for having lip-synched the Grammy-winning tune.

The thirty-four trustees of the National Academy of Recording Arts and Sciences, who awarded the Grammy, were furious. A telephone poll of the trustees indicated that they agreed that the award should be revoked, and—before the duo had a chance to return the award—the Academy stripped them of their Grammy. The Academy also decided that the revoked Grammy would not be awarded to anyone that year.

P. T. BARNUM HOAXES

Phineas Taylor Barnum (1810-1891) founded the circus in America. A master showman, he also authored a number of hoaxes, most of which were in good fun, and many of which were designed to raise money and garner publicity.

Circus Showman Scammed Scores of Unsuspecting Spectators!

The exhibition of Joice Heth was one of Barnum's earliest hoaxes. In the 1830s, the father of the American circus had an agreement for the rights to exhibit Heth, who was touted as being more than 160 years old and was supposed to have been George Washington's nurse. When Joice Heth died in 1836, an autopsy was performed. The story—published in an 1836 newspaper—claimed that she was not 161 years old at the time of her death. Another story, however—in the February 27, 1836, edition of the New York

Herald—claimed that the autopsied body was not really the body of Joice Heth; the real Heth, it seems, was still being exhibited in Connecticut.

In truth, the hoax was really on the *Herald*, which had been supplied with false information by Barnum's assistant, Levi Lyman. When confronted with his error Lyman agreed to supply the *Herald* with the real story of Joice Heth. This ran in six articles in the *Herald* beginning on September 8, 1836. As it turned out, this story, too, was a hoax. Lyman claimed that Barnum had discovered an elderly black woman on a Kentucky plantation, had her teeth extracted, taught her all about George Washington, and gradually raised her age as he exhibited her. Over a short period of time, Heth's age crept from 110 to 121, to 141, to 161 years old—a ripe old age for a southern plantation worker.

Barnum revealed in his autobiography that the story had been a figment of his assistant's fertile imagination; in actuality, Barnum had purchased the rights to exhibit Heth for ten months for $1,000. After opening an exhibit in New York City—with Lyman as the "barker"—Barnum was soon raking in some $1,500 per week. It was his first success in show business. When, after a while, the New York crowds began to dwindle, Barnum took Heth on the road to tour in New England cities.

Then Heth died unexpectedly. When the autopsy report indicated that Heth could not have been more than eighty years old, Lyman planted his "wrong body" story in the *Herald*, claiming that the person who had been autopsied was an elderly woman named "Aunt Nelly." With that, Barnum's 161-year-old woman hoax expired, but not before he had reaped more than $10,000 in profits.

A diminutive general. Barnum was not above using hoaxes to promote his otherwise legitimate acts. General Tom Thumb was the name Barnum gave to Charles Sherwood Stratton, an American-born midget. Stratton, a Connecticut native, was not a general of any sort. One of Barnum's most successful publicity coups came when Tom married another midget, Lavinia (Minnie) Warren. Some time later, Barnum had their picture taken holding a seven-pound baby; in reality, however, the couple, was childless. The child soon disappeared from the scene.

There's No Business Like Show Business

The long and short of it:
P. T. Barnum and
General Tom Thumb.

Good Sports
and
Sore Losers

World's Greatest Athletes

ABNER DOUBLEDAY AND THE HISTORY OF BASEBALL

The Baseball Hall of Fame in Cooperstown, New York, honors Abner Doubleday as the man who invented the game of baseball. Few people know much about Doubleday. Fewer still—least of all Doubleday himself—know why his name has been written into the history of America's national pastime.

Baseball's Founding Father Taken Out of the Ball Game!

Born in upstate New York in 1819, Doubleday attended West Point Academy (a military school) and was commissioned into the United States Army. After serving in battles in the Mexican War, he was promoted to the rank of major by 1861. Doubleday fired the first shot from Fort Sumter against the Confederates in the attack that began the Civil War.

By 1862, he had been promoted to major general, and he played a role in several important Civil War battles including Bull Run (second), Antietam, Fredricksburg, and Gettysburg. He spent the remainder of the war in Washington, D.C., and was eventually promoted to colonel after the war ended. In 1873, Colonel Doubleday retired from the service and moved to New Jersey. He died twenty years later and was buried in Arlington National Cemetery.

The special baseball commission report. A special baseball commission was set up in 1906 in order to establish whether baseball was an American invention. Charged with tracing the early history of the game,

Good Sports and Sore Losers

Abner Doubleday.

the commission of baseball experts made their report the following year. Intended as a history of the sport, it turned out to be quite a work of fiction.

The report claimed that Doubleday, while at school in Cooperstown in 1839, created the game of baseball out of the various forms of bat-

DOUBLEDAY'S SUPPOSED CONTRIBUTIONS TO BASEBALL

Albert Spaulding (the sporting goods giant), who hoped to prove that baseball was as American as apple pie, relied in part on the statements of Abner Graves, an elderly man living in Denver, Colorado. Graves stated in writing that he was sure that Doubleday had invented the game.

As a student at Green's Select School in Cooperstown in 1839, Doubleday—according to Graves—had improved Town Ball, the game that the students played at that time. Here is what, according to the elderly man from Denver, Doubleday contributed to baseball:

- Definite teams or sides were chosen.
- Each side was given eleven players.
- Four bases—where players could rest—were placed around a diamond.
- A pitcher was assigned to a six-foot ring in the center of the diamond.
- The game was called "Base Ball."

The story seems plausible enough, except for the fact that Doubleday was at West Point in 1839.

and-ball games called "one old cat" that were popular at that time. The commission concluded that Abner Doubleday, who would have been twenty years old in 1839, designed the diamond-shaped playing field, devised definite playing positions, and even thought up the name of "baseball."

Baseball—not an American game? Henry Chadwick—who was the first real baseball reporter and came to be known as "the Father of Baseball"—believed that the sport did not originate in the United States. Born in England, he claimed that he clearly remembered playing a British game known as rounders when he was a child.

Rounders had appeared in America at least a century before 1839, the year the special baseball commission claimed baseball had been invented. Chadwick believed that rounders probably derived from cricket, a bat-and-ball game that has a very long history in England. "Town ball," an American version of rounders, eventually led to the game of baseball. Printed rules for rounders existed in England in 1829, and rules for the game—under the name of "baseball"—can be traced back to 1834 in the United States. It looks like baseball, played like modern baseball, was first played in New York City in 1842. Rules for the game, however, were not formalized until 1845.

A deliberate hoax. Today, there is no doubt that the story that Abner Doubleday invented baseball was a deliberate hoax. Why was this West Point graduate and Civil War veteran named as the man who invented baseball? No one's telling. But Cooperstown is still honored as the place where the game was invented, and, to the general public, Doubleday retains his title as the inventor of baseball.

ROSIE RUIZ AND THE BOSTON MARATHON

The Boston Marathon is a twenty-six-mile, 385-yard foot race, held once a year in April. The 1980 women's division winner—with the third best time ever of two hours, thirty-one minutes, fifty-six seconds—was

Rosie Ruiz's fifteen minutes of fame.

Rosie Ruiz. At race's end, Ruiz, then a twenty-six-year-old administrative assistant from New York City, was immediately crowned with the winner's wreath.

Fleet-Footed Rosie Ruiz Races to Fishy Finale!

No sooner had Rosie donned the winner's wreath than skeptics began to question her victory. Why hadn't anyone seen her among the leaders of the race during the critical period before the final mile? How could Ruiz run so fast in Boston when—six months earlier—she had finished *663rd*, in twenty-fourth place among the women, in the New York Marathon? And why didn't Rosie look extremely tired after her twenty-six-mile stroll through Beantown?

The evidence was mounting, and Ruiz wasn't smelling like a rose. Several witnesses insisted that they had seen Jacqueline Gareau—the second-place finisher—leading the women all along, with Patti Lyons in second place. Several sportscasters who were commenting on the race for radio and TV also said they had not seen Ruiz near the front of the pack, if they saw her at all. And two runners assigned by WGBH-TV in Boston to watch for the lead man and woman at the halfway point both

> ### RUNNER-UP
>
> Jacqueline Gareau of Montreal, Canada, the 203rd person to finish the race, was the second woman to cross the finish line. She claimed that the first time she saw Rosie Ruiz was when she saw Rosie sitting with the winner's wreath on her head.

said that they never saw Rosie Ruiz. Nonetheless, several witnesses did say that they had seen Ruiz at the twenty-five-mile point in the women's lead and at other points in the race.

Public transportation gets you where you're going—faster. Although Ruiz said that she would be willing to take a lie detector test, none was given. But Rosie's athletic history was beginning to rewrite itself. A woman by the name of Susan Morrow came forward to say that she had met Rosie Ruiz on the subway in New York City—*during* the 1979 New York City Marathon. She said that she had ridden with Ruiz—who was wearing a contestant's uniform—from the ten-mile point of the race to Columbus Circle, near the finish; she also said that she walked with Ruiz to the finish line. Ruiz, it seems, had qualified for the Boston Marathon based on a race she never finished.

Rosie misses roll call. Ruiz denied ever having met Morrow, but the evidence continued to stack up against her. Officials of the Boston Marathon, who had compiled five lists of runners in the lead during the first twenty-four miles, pointed out that Rosie Ruiz's name did not appear on any of the lists. Finally, two Harvard students settled the Beantown disagreement: It seems they had seen Ruiz jump back into the race less than a mile from the finish. A seven-day intensive investigation and the review of more than 10,000 photographs of the race failed to show Rosie Ruiz at any point before the final mile. In the end—stripped of her New York Marathon time and deposed from her Boston crown—Rosie Ruiz lost more than a foot race.

THE CASE OF SIDD FINCH

Sportswriter George Plimpton told the story of Hayden (Sidd) Finch in the April 1, 1985, issue of *Sports Illustrated*. Finch, it seems, was a baseball pitcher who was able to throw a fastball at 168 miles per hour. During spring training at the New York Mets camp in St. Petersburg, Florida, the six-foot-four, twenty-eight year old was considered a pitching prodigy.

Brawny Brit Fires Fabulous Fastball!

Although Finch was from England, he had perfected his fastball during several years of practice in Tibet. His father, an archaeologist, had been killed in a plane crash in Nepal. After dropping out of Harvard after one semester, Finch was spotted by Mets scout Bob Schaefer in Maine, where Finch was playing for the Mets' AAA Farm Club. Schaefer, dumbfounded by the speed and accuracy of Finch's fastball, invited him to appear at the St. Petersburg spring training camp. Finch insisted on secrecy and several other conditions, and the Mets agreed.

Scams Illustrated. Plimpton's article was heavily illustrated with photos of Finch and Mets players and trainers taken in St. Petersburg. Readers—especially sports writers—were, in a word, intrigued. Plimpton, it seems, had decided, along with Mark Mulvoy, the editor of *Sports Illustrated,* to publish the magazine's first April Fool's article. Plimpton came up with the subject, the real Mets agreed to allow photographs to be taken at their spring training camp in St. Petersburg, and the fabulous Finch was portrayed by a friend of

---

A LOST PHOTO OPPORTUNITY

Four hundred and forty-nine women competed in the 1980 Boston Marathon. Race monitors had stationed photographers at six checkpoints along the route, where they were to photograph the leading **runners**—not specifically the leading **women**. Since 146 men finished ahead of Ruiz, the photographs of the leaders at each checkpoint showed only men runners. But that wouldn't be the only reason why Rosie missed out on a Kodak moment.

SILVER-PENNED HOAXER

Plimpton's article was so well written that there was scarcely a clue that it was a hoax. Almost no one had noticed that the first letter of each word in the introduction of the original article spelled a secret message:

He's a pitcher, part yogi and part recluse. Impressively liberated from our opulent life-style, Sidd's deciding about yoga and his future in baseball.

The message was: "H-A-P-P-Y-A-P-R-I-L-F-O-O-L-S-D-A-Y."

Phoney Finch winding up for the pitch.

the photographer; although his real name was not recorded, some people believe that he was a school teacher from Chicago.

Sports Illustrated finally unveiled the hoax after having received a deluge of phone calls about Finch from readers. The April 8 issue of *SI* reported that Finch had lost his pinpoint accuracy; following a press conference, the prodigious pitcher simply waved to the crowd and walked away from baseball forever.

VICTOR NOTARO'S SOCCER STORIES

In March 1982, thousands of Canadians were thrilled to read about an Ontario teenager who led the Canadian junior soccer team to victory in a World Cup championship in Sydney, Australia. Victor Notaro was that teenager, and the whole story was an elaborate hoax.

Good Sports and Sore Losers

Canadian Teenager Seeks Sports Trophy—
the World Cup!

Notaro began by sending information from Kalamazoo, Michigan—where he attended college—to his hometown newspaper in Canada. The material included information about the upcoming tournament in February, and Notaro's role on the Canadian team that would be playing in Australia. Canada beat West Germany, Brazil, and the Soviet Union—all with the hoaxer's help—and Notaro provided telephone reports of each victory to the local newspaper, the *Welland* [Ontario] *Tribune*. After the *Tribune* passed the information on to the Canadian Press Agency, newspapers all over Canada picked up the news of the spectacular success of the Canadian soccer team.

Soon, however, some of the other papers checked into the story and found that the tournament did not exist. Confronted by reporters, Notaro admitted that he made up the story; he was just a hometown boy looking for a local sports trophy.

INDEX

Boldface indicates entrants

DATE DUE

APR 20 1999	